D1827482

Behind a Painted Smile

About a woman who hides all the hurt, pain, fears and emotions that life has thrown at her. She hides behind a false face, being her painted smile.

by

Rosie Shannon

authorHOUSE®

AuthorHouse™ UK Ltd.
500 Avebury Boulevard
Central Milton Keynes, MK9 2BE
www.authorhouse.co.uk
Phone: 08001974150

First published by AuthorHouse 12/21/2007

ISBN: 978-1-4343-4521-9 (sc)

Printed in the United States of America
Bloomington, Indiana

This book is printed on acid-free paper.

Dedicated to the memory of Daniel, my eldest son.

'Precious is the time we spent together
Loving you always, forgetting you never.'

CHAPTER ONE ───────────────

As 2003 drew to a close I began the difficult task of building a new life. I was certain that Daniel, my late son, was giving me the strength to look at myself in a positive way, rather than dwelling on the turmoil and heartbreak of the past. For me, starting over again is about creating a positive self-image, letting the world see the real face of Rosie Shannon that has for so long remained hidden behind a painted smile.

Even though the psychological effects of the physical and sexual abuse my brother inflicted on me throughout my childhood and teenage years will never go away, I had to move on. The awful memory of Daniel's death in a road accident still haunts me, yet I must learn to live with it. Although these terrible things remain deeply embedded in my subconscious I am becoming stronger in dealing with them when they surface. Not being as naive as I once was has helped me develop a clearer view of life.

From this point I made a decision to focus on reality rather than pretence and I chose to concentrate on strengths rather than weaknesses. For example, my singing voice improved to the point where I could perform in public with greater confidence than ever before, mainly at local karaoke evenings, but it still meant facing an audience. When I first began my singing lessons I would face the wall, turning away from my voice coach. I couldn't look at her when I sang, whether it was embarrassment or just a lack of confidence I wasn't sure, but things have certainly improved in that department.

I will always believe that Daniel's spirit continues to guide me and he is the one I turn to in times of difficulty. A young woman working in one of the shops in Retford, my hometown, knew this and gave me the telephone number of a spiritualist medium called Michael of whom she spoke very highly. I made an appointment to see him. At my appointment he put me at ease before producing a set of coloured ribbons from which he asked me to choose a selection. From my choice he was able to see into my life and everything he told me was true. He knew about the pain my father had suffered before he died, about my traumatic upbringing and about my brother abusing me. He even told me that my son Daniel's life had been cut short, but had sent me a message saying, "everything would be alright". Even now, if I'm concerned about anything, I know that I can telephone this man, and he will advise me what to do.

Monday 8th June 2004

I have crossed my next hurdle. A young singer, who I know well, was performing in a local pub and she asked me if I wanted to sing on the same bill. I felt quite apprehensive at first because all I have done so far is karaoke and as there wouldn't be any words to help me, I had to choose a song where I was word perfect.

I watched the clock all through her performance and by the time she had finished her act it was late. She thanked everyone for coming and I thought, "that's it, it's too late for me to go on", but then she looked in my direction and beckoned; heads turned in expectation. I had chosen to sing "Somewhere Over the Rainbow" (which I had previously recorded on an album in memory of Daniel). She asked if I was ready to start and then panic took over, she calmed me down and assured me that once I heard the music I would be fine.

She picked up the microphone and asked the audience to be quiet and then announced that I was going to dedicate the song to Daniel who had recently died. I was shaking so much and inwardly begging Daniel to help me. The music began, my throat tightened and I was still shaking. The audience went quiet and I began to sing. I was scared that I would forget the words and let Daniel down but I finished the song, I have no idea how, and I do believe that Daniel was with me all the way.

Not knowing what to expect, I turned the microphone off and nervously faced the crowd. There was applause, people wept and someone even had to go outside. My song had gone straight to the heart. I was near to tears when John (my ex partner, who was in the audience) took hold of me for support.

I proved to someone else who's birthday it would have been today that I am a stronger person than she ever thought I could be, my mother (who is dead).

Wednesday 16th June 2004

My first book hasn't been printed yet; I need to be patient for few more weeks. I picked up my mail from the front porch this morning and among the letters I received was one from my publisher containing a draft cover for my book. I didn't know whether to laugh or cry - I was excited, emotional and very proud too.

The cover is just perfect; it not only illustrates the desolation of my childhood but also the loneliness that has typified my adult years. I phoned the publisher as soon as I could to let him know I had received it, and how pleased I am. I can't wait to see the book in its finished form.

It seems strange that I can be so excited about a book that describes events in my life that are shocking and in some cases horrific. I wish they hadn't happened but you can't turn back the clock. I know from experience that living in the present will always be influenced by what has happened in the past. For example, this afternoon I was getting ready to go into town to choose flowers for Daniel's grave (on 22nd June it will be the

3rd anniversary of his death), and my mood was at its lowest ebb when the telephone rang. It was my publisher who was ringing with the news that my book has just been allocated an I.S.B.N. number. This means that my work will now be available for sale not just locally but nationally. I was really emotional and had to fight back the tears; I wanted to tell the world. I thanked him, though I don't think I made much sense as I was speaking too quickly.

I have been working really hard on the material for my second album. I am performing two duets with Tim (a young local singer who is away at college) as well as the solo tracks. By the time Tim returns home to Retford, my solo tracks should be complete. Working with Tim is a delight because he is so talented, he performed on my first album and I wouldn't want to sing with anyone else.

I am now waiting anxiously for 21st June, as that is when Daniel's anniversary flowers are going to be delivered. I have chosen a blue heart with a white ribbon border this year with Daniel's initial in the centre surrounded by white carnations. I am planning to take them to the cemetery the day before his anniversary, as it will be too painful to go there on the actual day.

It is my youngest daughter's birthday today (she lives in Scotland) and as each year passes it brings back so many memories. I won't send a card or a present; it will be too confusing for her (even though we keep in touch).

Sunday 20th June 2004

I went out with a good friend today to a local pub where he runs the karaoke. I sung a lot and as the evening drew to an end he let me sing one more song. He knew it was getting close to Daniel's 3rd anniversary and he let me choose a song, he probably knew that I would choose "Angels" by Robbie Williams as it was Daniel's favourite.

This song evokes strong emotions, as it was the one I'd played as people were arriving at his funeral. As many of the customers in the pub were strangers to me, my friend explained why I'd chosen to sing that particular song. Afterwards people applauded and some, who I had never met, came and shook my hand before leaving.

Monday 21st June 2004

I have not been looking forward to today. It is the day before Daniel's anniversary.

I was next door at my friend's house when the florist delivered the flowers; they had done a beautiful job. My friend, who drove me to the cemetery, had bought some new flowerpots for each side of the headstone. When we got there I cleaned everything and gently placed the flowers in position.

In the tranquil setting of the cemetery Daniel's grave looked beautiful but all I could feel inside was the turmoil of sadness, anger and pain. These feelings will always be there, below the surface, ready to emerge at times like this. I guess every mother who has lost a child in whatever circumstances will know the same feelings.

I have a new digital camera and took many photographs of the grave; these were for an album I am keeping just for Daniel. To my horror, on returning home, I plugged the camera into the computer and there were no photographs, just a blank screen. So, I ate some humble pie and turned to John for help. When our relationship ended he removed most of his things from the house, except for his camera. I phoned him and explained what had happened and he called round at the house, picked up his camera and went to the cemetery to photograph Daniel's grave for me.

This was a wonderful gesture from someone I had previously ejected from my life.

Tuesday 22nd June 2004

Lying in bed last night I cried until no more tears would fall, I waited for midnight to pass and for Daniel's 3rd anniversary - I felt so alone. I knew I had come this far and must pull myself together. I had to be strong as I prepared myself for an emotional day.

At approximately midday my publisher phoned to let me know he'd found a printing company for my book. The proofs will go to print on the 23rd June. I was delighted, this was just the tonic I needed; I said to him, "I hope Danny's watching." What an achievement to hear that your first book is going to print - the feeling is wonderful. I just couldn't believe it.

About an hour later, John called with the photographs he'd taken of Daniel's flowers; they were perfect.

I must say for the rest of the day my phone never stopped ringing. It was finally happening, I had written a book, a back street girl who'd left school with just a basic education. I feel I have come so far. I have to let my friends know that it will only be a few weeks before the launch at Bookworm (The Retford Bookshop).

Since writing my first book, I have developed an even greater passion for putting my feelings and emotions onto paper. There may be a few people who aren't happy with what I'm doing but the days of being dictated to are gone. I make my own decisions now.

July 6th and 7th 2004

I am back in the studio to begin recording my second album but I have to wait until the backing tracks for the rest of my songs are ready. I also have to wait for my singing partner Tim to come home to do the duets with me. I've been amazed by the change in my voice in less than a year, it has matured and the album will hopefully turn out really well. I am actually having fun doing it.

Wednesday July 14th 2004.

Today I received a phone call from my publisher telling me that he will be collecting the proofs and book cover from the printers. I can't believe they are finally ready. My feelings are of excitement and joy.

I know my publisher is going on holiday and so I will have to wait until he returns before a launch date can be finalised. I suppose I'm a little frightened of the unknown but I have to get used to everything an author has to do. Getting a book published is not the end of it. Marketing is crucial to a book's success and I know that I will have to do my bit to ensure that it sells. Friends and people I know have been supportive about the book but I suppose to them it could all be a kind of make believe on my part until they actually see it in the bookshop.

Saturday 17ᵗʰ July 2004

John stayed last night. I agreed that he and some of his friends could come around today for a buffet lunch. I've not met them before and they were really nice. The day was great and we had lots of fun.

John and I decided to spend the evening at a local pub (where I go most weekends). He asked if he could stay over and like an idiot I agreed. The next day thing's changed, John's attentiveness towards me cooled. Whatever feelings we had generated for each other had disappeared. To him it was just a physical thing; he had to satisfy his own need. When I asked if I would be seeing him again he told me our relationship had ended sometime ago and we were now only good friends. I was very bitter and angry with myself. I felt used.

Saturday 24thJuly 2004

Surprise, surprise, John contacted me, wanting us to get back together. A week ago we were just good friends, so why this sudden change of heart? Eventually the truth emerged.

John wants me to move out of the house (which I rent from him). His friends who had been round for the buffet were staying with him and he wanted them to leave. They have got two children and things are becoming difficult. The meal was just a ploy to allow them to get a good look at the house. His plan was that I would move out allowing his friends to move in.

I phoned Michael (my spiritualist friend), who confirmed my worst fears. He told me not to move, as I would be the one out on the street. I have certain rights as a tenant and legally John can't force me to leave. The thought of being homeless doesn't appeal to me and so I am staying put.

Tuesday 27th July 2004

Knowing he can't evict me, John has asked the couple and their children to leave his home, thus ending their friendship. There was a time when I would have meekly done as John wanted but I am in charge of my own life now. This is my home and for as long as I pay the rent that's how it will stay.

I have been recording and was in my element as it all went really well but just as the session ended I received a text message from the woman John had invited for a buffet at my house. The text said that he'd been lying to me and not to trust him, especially if he tried to resume our relationship. When I read the next part of her message, I was devastated. It said that he'd slept with a friend of hers who is only seventeen years old.

I walked to the taxi office where John works as a driver and my anger began to rise. He drove me home and on the way I read the message again. John asked me what it said but I wouldn't tell him. I broached him with the same question that I'd asked two weeks previously, "have you slept with anyone else?" He told me he hadn't. I then said "does a seventeen year old mean anything to you?" He knew that he had no option but to tell me. He said that the couple had set it all up. I was totally sickened by this as she was still a child, though John said he thought she was in her twenties. When I asked John why he lied to me, he said he didn't want to hurt my feelings. I kept my feelings to myself so that John wouldn't know how much I was hurting.

John said that although they slept together in the same bed, nothing intimate took place, as he was drunk at the time. He explained what did and did not take place. I suppose I believed him because of the amount of time I had known him.

In a strange way this episode has brought us closer. I began to open up and feel more at ease with John, something which I hadn't done in nearly two and a half years. Perhaps I felt sorry for him.

The last time I confided in John was when I gave statements to the police about my brother's abusive behaviour towards me. Although things still weren't perfect between us, it almost seemed that we had never been away from each other. Now I could talk to John about my feelings whereas before we couldn't talk at all.

Friday 6ᵗʰ August 2004

I phoned my publisher today to see if there had been any progress on my book and he explained there is always progress with any book. He has the final proofs with him, made up in their cover. I told him he was a "jammy devil", as I hadn't seen my work in its final form.

I am still anxious for a launch date for my book but my publisher has told me it will be about ten days following return of the proofs to the printer that the book would be ready. Even though I can't use that as an exact date, at least I now have an idea of how much longer it will be. One thing is certain; I know my book will be perfect.

I am staying overnight at John's house tonight, even though I am still unsure of his motives. Maybe I'm too busy to see the real truth, or maybe I don't want to.

Friday 13ᵗʰ August 2004

Recording again, only this time with Tim who is back home from college. Tim has a wonderful voice yet he doesn't boast about it. I was nervous about the session.

The songs we'd chosen were really difficult but we patiently worked through them. We recorded the songs on to discs but they haven't been mixed yet, this is left to the studio technicians; we take no part in it. I was pleasantly surprised at the way our duets turned out; Tim is such a brilliant singer.

I have two more songs to record and then be patient until the finished album is ready. What with the book and the album I should be satisfied but I want something else to keep me going.

Saturday 28th August 2004

I phoned Sandra (my spiritualist friend's wife) to make enquiries about weekly group meetings held at her church. She explained that different mediums attended and any links or messages from the spirit world were more likely to come through if the recipients were in the audience. I decided to attend tonight. I was nervous but once I'd joined company with Sandra and Michael, I felt calmer. Even though no messages came through for me, the evening was interesting. On reflection, I know that I have to carry on going each week.

The excitement of waiting for the publication of my book is driving me crazy. I visit my friend next door every day; she's a great listener and I tell her everything. For people like me, who have experienced devastating trauma in their lives, friends who take time to listen are truly a Godsend. Often what is not fully understood is the need to keep talking things out. This valuable part of the healing process can only be accomplished if there is someone who has the time and patience to listen.

Another such friend owns a shop, intriguingly called "Mystique", in Retford town centre. Her name is Clair and I like and love everything about her. She doesn't judge me but takes me for the person I am. It was Clair who put me in touch with Michael and between the two of them they have always made time to talk, putting my mind at ease and regularly assuring me that things will turn out well.

Wednesday 1ˢᵗ September 2004

I phoned my publisher, he was out but his wife thought that as yesterday was a public holiday there wouldn't be any news on my book. I felt down and disappointed. Approximately half an hour later my phone rang, it was my publisher and his words were "your books are ready." I could not believe it. All my gloomy feelings disappeared and I laughed and cried at the same time.

The adrenaline running through my body was unreal. I couldn't thank him enough, I was so grateful. He told me he is going to collect the books tomorrow and asked me to meet him as he wanted to hand over my author's copies personally. We have agreed to meet for coffee at a small teashop in Carolgate.

Thursday 2nd September 2004

I met my publisher today as we agreed yesterday on the phone. When I arrived he was outside waiting for me and in his hand was a white envelope. My mind went back to the Christmases of my childhood. This particular Santa Claus was bringing me the best present I had ever had.

We sat down with our drinks. My big achievement day had finally arrived. With trembling hands I opened the package and there were two copies of my very own book. I remember saying I could not believe I'd done it, I had at long last written a book and had it published. I reached into my handbag for a tissue; to say I was overjoyed would be an understatement.

The book has mirrored my life inasmuch that it had not been a smooth transition from the original manuscript to final publication. There have been both legal and family problems to surmount. I have been worried what the general public's reaction will be once it goes on sale, especially from people who know me. Now, with the book in front of me I have fulfilled my one dream in life, to be honest, open and tell the world about how my life has really been. It is such a relief that I will never again have to lie about my past to people or to pretend any longer.

Between us, my publisher and I have worked out some dates for a book signing; everything is happening at speed. We made our way across to Bookworm (where the book is going on sale) and together with the bookshop owners we have settled for 10 am on Friday 10th September for the launch. This will be my day of fame. It will be a day just for myself.

Arriving back home I had to catch my breath. The pace at which things are happening is frightening - I am about to enter the unknown. This is something my publisher warned me about, he said "it will be on you before you know it." Believe me, he is right.

CHAPTER TWO ─────────────

From that day my publisher arranged for the posters to be printed and displayed in the bookshop window. It was my job to notify local newspapers. I knew that after all these years I was ready for my story to be heard. I just wanted the world to know.

I was immensely proud of what I'd achieved. I took photographs of the shop and the poster, which told the world when my book signing would be. Seeing my name on a book was emotional but to see my name on a publicly displayed poster evoked a special feeling. Even so, I still could not believe what would become of it all. There was no way of predicting how the public would react, especially people who knew me.

As the time leading up to the launch became shorter, I surprised myself by staying calm, relaxed and some would say quite laid back about it all. The evening before, I began to question myself. What if I'm not dressed appropriately, or my manner of speaking is not up to standard. How would I answer questions from the public? Any self-doubt had to be hidden. I decided to just be myself and then I wouldn't go far wrong.

Friday 10th September 2004

My big day has arrived. At 6.30 a.m. the alarm clock startled me but I was already awake. Convinced that I would be nervous it came as a surprise that I felt quite calm and began my day with a hot drink and a light breakfast.

Even though it was two hours before my big event I felt as if nothing different was happening, perhaps I was fooling myself. As far as I was aware my behaviour was normal, but it couldn't have been because Alfie (my cat) kept her distance. I learnt a long time ago that she responds to whatever mood I'm in. This time she must have detected a rather anxious owner, even though I tried not to show it. (Incidentally, as a kitten I mistakenly thought "she" was a "he" so I named her Alfie. She doesn't seem to mind.)

There were things to prepare so I arranged to meet my publisher inside Bookworm at about half past nine. My cuckoo clock reminded me that I had to get a move on, so following a final check in the mirror, when I almost convinced myself that my outfit was suitable for the occasion, I dropped the catch and popped in to see my friend next door. I felt a bit emotional but was determined not to cry, as it would ruin my make up. I wasn't ready to come out from behind my mask just yet. I looked at her and asked, "Do I look alright?" She assured me that I looked great, which put my mind at ease.

Between talking to her and waiting for my taxi, I nearly wore out the living room carpet. I prayed that my taxi would be on time; sure enough it arrived as planned at quarter past nine. The driver asked if I was nervous, I told him I was OK though already I could feel a mixture of excitement and anxiety building up. This was a day for keeping cool so I kept my feelings hidden.

I arrived early at Bookworm; my publisher hadn't yet put in an appearance. There were two biros on the table where I would be signing but I had brought my own. My friend next door had given me a stylish Parker for luck. She said I shouldn't be signing my book with any old pen. This was a day to be proud; I'd spent time and money on my appearance so why spoil it by signing my name with a cheap pen. What surprised me was that I felt different to how I expected to feel. I thought I would be uptight, quiet and shy but I was completely the opposite.

My publisher arrived, complimented me on my appearance then checked that my book was properly displayed. Copies were fanned out on the table, inviting people to pick them up. It was nearly ten o'clock when a lady came in and asked if I'd started yet. She seemed to be trouble so even though it was not quite time to start I said "yes". Hers was the first book I signed, with a small dedication saying that I hoped it would give her some comfort.

The next person to arrive in the shop was a photographer from The Retford Times newspaper. She put me at ease, commenting on how nice I looked. Michael had always assured me that everything would be alright where my book was concerned. Of course I still had doubts as nothing ever seems to go right for me in life. Clair also told me time and again that it would be a success. Both Michael and Clair are so supportive words cannot thank them enough.

Clair was the next person to come into the shop. She gave me a reassuring hug and a beautiful bouquet of flowers with a congratulations card. She then bought three books. Following Clair's visit I felt stronger. John my ex-partner came in and bought a book, which was something I never thought he would do. I found that some of the customers stayed to talk and others just wanted a copy signed or dedicated. I felt quite happy and calm, feeling as if I had done this before, but I knew I hadn't. It just felt so natural.

My publisher went for his lunch but I decided to stay in the bookshop in case I missed anyone calling in during the lunch break. A few books sold whilst he was away and on his return he decided to go back to the office as other work was pressing. He said that authors usually stay for a few hours then leave, which is what he thought I would do. I thought otherwise and decided to stay longer. The bookshop owners agreed to this.

Having signed ten copies of my book I left them on the display table then allowed myself thirty minutes for lunch. I also made time to call in to see Clair to tell her how well things were going. On my return there were only four copies left. I was speechless; I knew that I had to stay much longer. Quite soon I was running out of books and my publisher had gone. His office was twenty miles away but following a phone call from the bookshop he delivered another consignment. I stayed until about five o'clock; sales were so brisk that everyone was taken by surprise. For a local book it had exceeded all expectations. The North Notts Guardian did a write up about the book signing which stimulated greater public interest. More deliveries were made to Bookworm where, for a while, it continued to sell very well.

During the time I was at lunch a member of staff from Victim Support bought my book. For me this was significant as she was the person who gave me professional and emotional support when it was most needed. It was during and after the court case involving my brother that she spent many hours on the telephone giving me the courage to carry on. Her name is Gina and I never did meet her face to face and even when she came into the bookshop I wasn't there. It would have been wonderful to thank her personally.

Another person who came into my life at that time was a W.P.C. based at Retford Police Station. She was the officer who dealt with the case against my brother and never once doubted my side of the story. A copy of my book with a special dedication was sent to her.

As part of my publisher's contract I received two free author's copies of my book. One of these I sent to my solicitor as a thank you gift. In the early stages of drafting my manuscript there had been a legal injunction taken out to prevent its publication. Without the professional help received from my solicitor the book would never have been published. Even so, a chapter had to be deleted which in hindsight was the proper thing to do.

Thursday 23rd September 2004.

My relationship with John is well and truly over but he still visits and phones me. Tonight he called to see me and we had an intensely fierce argument. Soon after John left the right side of my body went icy cold and the atmosphere in the house became strange. Two of the clocks had lost time and one of the alarms went off. There was no reason for this as the clock had not even been set. Feeling scared and unsafe I panicked, I phoned Michael but he was out and Sandra offered to come and see me.

We sat and talked, I explained what had happened and she told me that it would be Daniel whose spirit was still in the house. He was angry with John for what he'd done and was also telling me it was time to move on, to go forward with my life. Sandra sat with me for about three hours and I spoke about my past in a way that I could never do with a doctor or counsellor. I was at ease with her knowing instinctively that I could trust her. Afterwards, I felt so much better; it was as if a huge weight had been lifted from my shoulders.

Friday 24th September 2004

This morning I received a telephone call from a man named Trevor who works for the police and also for victim support. During the time when my brother's case was going through the courts he came to my house where he fitted additional locks to the doors and windows. He installed an intruder alarm and several smoke alarms too. These precautions became necessary because there was always the possibility of my brother threatening me with violence or other forms of intimidation in an attempt to frighten me into withdrawing my complaint. Thankfully, this didn't happen.

Trevor said that he would be buying two copies of my book and would I dedicate them to himself and Sally, another Victim Support worker. Of course I agreed. Not all people who have experienced serious sexual abuse want to write about it. Perhaps my book would be useful in helping Trevor and Sally to further understand the long-term psychological harm that is done to people in this situation, I certainly hoped so.

My publisher told me that local books such as mine have to be marketed in different ways. One quite effective way is for the author to give public talks based on their book including the motivation behind it, problems encountered along the way to publication and so on. Never having done this before and after much persuasion, I agreed.

The Denman Library in Retford would be the venue for the first of these. Later that day I delivered posters advertising my talk to various places around the town, as well as leaving one at the library. Bookworm put a poster in their window, as did my friend Clair. The North Notts Trader newspaper published a short piece in its editorial section; a poster also appeared in the Trader office front window.

Later that afternoon, a knock came at my door. It was Trevor. How wonderful it was to see him again, he has such a great personality. Throughout my ordeal, no matter how low I was feeling, he would always manage to make me smile. We talked for some time, I dedicated both the books he had bought and also wrote a note to Gina who I had missed at the book launch. I owe the people from Victim Support so much. They are all very special.

Tuesday 28th September 2004

I had been out of bed for just over an hour when I realised my rib cage and one side of my neck and back had begun to feel painful. I could not understand it; I hadn't got a cough, I wasn't off my food yet the pain was increasing. I managed to get a doctor's appointment for the evening by which time the pain had gone into my chest. He examined me and as I attempted to get up my legs buckled. According to my doctor a virus that had been around since the turn of the 20th century, when there had been a serious epidemic, had infected me. He gave me strong painkillers and prescribed total rest for at least two weeks.

Never before have I felt this ill, normal conversation left me unable to breathe. Evidently this strain of virus attacks the soft tissue of the body and even the slightest exertion causes excruciating pain; I was left exhausted and breathless. I have no idea where it came from.

Friday1st October 2004

Tomorrow would have been Daniels 22nd birthday, but I still cannot bring myself to visit the cemetery on the anniversary of his birth. I always go the day before, that way I am usually the first one to put flowers on his grave.

Clair asked if there was anything she or her husband John could do to help, particularly as I was unwell. It is not my nature to put on people or feel that I am using them but Clair was insistent. I accepted and asked if they would mind taking me to the cemetery with Daniel's flowers.

Some time ago Clair suffered a badly broken arm and is unable to drive and so John called at my house and took me to the cemetery. I was pleased that no one had been before me, which meant the world to me. On returning home I felt a sense of relief as yet another hurdle had been cleared. Anyone who thinks things become easier could not be more mistaken. Questions still linger in the mind. What did Daniel do to deserve to be killed? Why was his life cut short? I admit tears are shed once I'm behind closed doors but deep inside I know that Daniel would not want me to cry for him.

Saturday October 2nd 2004

I woke earlier than usual. Looking across my bedroom at Daniel's photograph I wished him happy birthday. I spoke out loud, telling him how much I would give just to turn the clock back, just to see him again. I hoped and prayed that he was somewhere close by, listening. Opening the top drawer of my dressing table I removed an envelope containing another, different photograph of Daniel. It was one taken by the undertaker. I had dressed Daniel for his funeral and as he lay in his coffin he looked so peaceful and serene. I broke down. Sobbing into my hands I asked the simple question "why?" It is the question that all parents who have lost a child ask over and over again. There is no answer.

Putting the picture away I went downstairs. Sitting in front of the clock I waited until the hands reached 10.15 am, the time of Daniel's birth. I played my recording of "Somewhere over the Rainbow", which was his song. Racked with emotion I prayed that he was just over that rainbow and it was a wonderful and better place for him.

Later, I went to the spiritualist church and a medium performing there came to me first. He told me that someone was giving me a birthday card. My facial expression must have betrayed total shock but inside I was jumping for joy. I just knew it was Daniel. Glancing across at Michael and Sandra I mouthed "Danny". They nodded. The spiritualist told me that I was trying to move forward but there was something holding me back.

When the evening ended Michael and Sandra offered to take me home. I told them about the photograph of Daniel secreted away in my dressing table drawer. Michael said it was something I should not have around me. Continually looking at it wasn't good for me. Daniel should be remembered with his beaming smile, full of life, not dead in a photograph. Although, at the time of his funeral, I thought it was the right thing to do, but Michael was making sense.

Michael and Sandra have the photograph now, they are looking after it for me. Michael said if I ever need to see it then I know where it is. That evening, with it being Daniel's birthday, they gave me flowers.

Tuesday 5th October 2004

Today I decided to telephone my friend in Scotland - the one who had adopted my daughters. I had sent her a copy of "More than I Deserved" and was curious to know her reaction. She thought it was an enjoyable read but there was a lot of missing detail. Leaving my daughters behind must have been heartbreaking and it was her view that I had not expressed my true feelings.

I had to admit she was right. To leave them behind was bad enough; I still have to live with that decision 24 hours a day, seven days a week. When I gave birth to them I was lucky. In each case I had a quick and easy labour. As I held them in my arms what pain there was soon disappeared from my mind. When I walked away from them I felt I was reliving the pain of their births all over again but the pain I felt inside was much more intense. It was gut wrenching, almost unbearable.

I have no idea whether the choice I made was right or wrong. Sometimes I look at other children and feel intense sadness, just wishing I had my girls to love, to care for and to be happy with. Yes, it does break my heart in ways that I cannot describe. However, as I explained to my friend, the book is about me not them. I had left my girls in the best possible care, with all the love they would ever need. They'd been given the chance of a better life, certainly one that I could never have given them.

My friend asked if I had ever undergone counselling for what happened to me when I was abused. I told her I hadn't because to me it would have been like an interrogation. I explained that I felt like a criminal who was being accused, yet I was the victim. I think she understood what I was saying and where I was coming from. She knew that I had sustained a lot of psychological damage that would never be completely healed. Like physical scars some mental scars remain forever.

Friday 8th October 2004.

My publisher is planning for me to speak about my book in public for the first time and because my talk would be at the Denman Library in Retford, the local newspaper was running a piece on it. I decided to telephone the newspaper office. I knew the girls quite well and one of them told me that the papers had just arrived. She told me what page the story was on and I asked if five copies could be put to one side. I telephoned John, asking him to collect the newspapers for me. Initially he was reluctant, saying he was too busy, yet within the hour he'd brought them to the house. The editor had certainly done a good job. The piece was accurate; it told readers that I did not deserve what had happened to me. I hope that the publicity will attract a good number of people to my talk scheduled for the 15th October.

Monday 11th October 2004.

Today presented a real challenge for me. Although my book is selling well I still have to find other ways for my work to help others who have suffered serious sexual abuse. Gina from Victim Support told me her article about my book was in their magazine, which she had posted to me. This would certainly help.

Following a discussion with my publisher I began contacting radio stations. The results were positive. One station agreed to send a reporter to my talk at the Retford library.

I then telephoned BBC Radio Nottingham, although courteous and helpful the woman I spoke to advised me that the presenter who usually covered my kind of story was on holiday, though she did ask for some information about my book. My publisher had E-mailed a press release yesterday evening and I can only assume that my phone call prompted them to read it because a short while later a person from BBC Radio Nottingham phoned me. They asked if I would go to the studio tomorrow at 3 pm, to be interviewed live on air from 3.15 until 3.35 pm.

This took me completely by surprise, I was in shock so much that I had to ask her what day it was, then asked her to give me 15 minutes as I had no idea how I was going to get there as I don't drive. I knew John wouldn't take me. This was too good an opportunity to miss so in a bit of a fluster I phoned my publisher who said he would take me himself.

The studio was informed that transport had been arranged and we would be there on time. I was asked to choose four favourite songs to be broadcast during the interview. I was also asked what my hobbies were and I said singing was one of them. When I mentioned the album I'd recorded last year in memory of Daniel they asked me to bring it with me.

The songs I have chosen for the Programme are, "Somewhere Over The Rainbow", "What If", "Baby Can I Hold You Tonight", and "Forever Love". Though I am not certain which "Somewhere Over The Rainbow" they will play, the original by Judy Garland or the one I had recorded.

Later I phoned my voice coach - she was really pleased. Although BBC Radio Nottingham said they would tape the interview for me my voice coach said she would also record it.

All this is new to me; it is difficult to imagine that so many people will hear about my life. I am really looking forward to it.

Wednesday 13th October 2004.

This is the big day. I was not nervous but spent some time arranging my clothes and jewellery just to keep busy. The post brought a letter with Crimestoppers printed on the front. I opened it with caution, not knowing what to expect. Official looking letters always give me the shakes, but I needn't have worried. It was a letter from Gina at Victim Support. Enclosed was a copy of the piece she had written about my book. I dabbed at the tears of happiness that pricked my eyes. I had put my first layer of make up on and didn't want to ruin it.

CHAPTER THREE ——————————

My publisher was collecting me at half past one. By 1 o'clock I was ready. I used the spare half hour to go next door. I needed reassurance that I looked presentable and smart enough. Anyone would think I was going on television but a girl has to look her best no matter what. My friend was just as excited as me. Then I began to pace up and down her living room carpet. The nerves were beginning to show. I had come this far; I had to see it through. My friend hugged me and I went back home to wait for my publisher to arrive. It seemed like hours but once in the car I just felt a sense of calm. Daniel was sending me the strength I needed.

On arrival at BBC Radio Nottingham the people were kind and caring, I felt completely at ease. Whilst in the building I had to wear a security tag. All this was new to me. Michaela, a staff member, showed me the studio where I would be interviewed. Then a young man chatted to me, offering reassurance that I would be alright. Nick, the Programme presenter then invited me into the studio. I asked Michaela to record the interview for me. She said she would. I was only supposed to have twenty minutes on air but it carried on for much longer lasting approximately forty minutes.

The presenter did not know much about my story so he asked random questions. I had to fill in the gaps. In places my emotions were struggling to get the better of me, the interview brought back so many painful memories. The musical interludes gave me breathing space and Nick told me how well I was doing, although I must admit to feeling less than confident at the time. After the interview Nick wished me good luck, he said what a fantastic interview it was.

Outside the studio Michaela was waiting with a young man, she gave me the recording and they both said how brave I was. They remarked how natural I sounded. Michaela said I had made the young man cry. He couldn't believe what I'd gone through. I thanked them all, saying how grateful I was to be given the opportunity to share my life experiences with so many people.

My publisher was waiting in his car; he'd listened to the interview on his radio and said that I was amazing. I thought that he was just saying that, but he is so honest and straight to the point. He said the interview was perfect. I was pleased not to have let him down or disappointed him as he really had put himself out a lot for me.

Thursday 14th October 2004

I went shopping today and everyone who I met in town stopped and congratulated me saying how well I had done. When I was in the supermarket I heard someone say, "Hi Rosie, how are you?"

I turned around and saw that it was the person who had lived next door when I was growing up and being abused. "Why didn't you say something to us," she said. The middle of a crowded supermarket is not the best place to have an intimate conversation so I said I would call her.

Friday 15th October 2004.

Today was the day for my talk at the local library. I thought that after my interview on BBC Radio Nottingham there would be a sizeable audience but not many people turned up. So I expressed my thanks to the small number that did attend.

I started to tell my story. At first I remained calm and in control but dragging those awful memories to the surface again, plus a feeling of sheer exhaustion, caused me to break down a few times. My painted smile became more tear-stained by the minute. When I looked around some of the audience were crying with me and when my talk was over one or two people stayed behind to ask questions and pass comment.

I went too deep into my story and I feel like I have let my publisher down. He said I had to learn to let people make their own connections and not to spell out everything to them. Well, as the old saying goes, "you learn from your mistakes" and after all this was my first attempt at public speaking. I took heart in the fact that any future talks would be better.

Sunday 24ᵗʰ October 2004

Today I tried out a different public house, as the one I usually frequented was not the same anymore. It did seem to have lost its attraction and I can't enjoy a night out when there are no people to enjoy it with. My new venue, The Albert Hotel, offered me a new atmosphere. Here I could enjoy myself. The karaoke was special and the people were different too. Some weekends they have live entertainment and my friend Nicola has been booked to sing next Saturday evening.

Saturday 30ᵗʰ October 2004

Nicola knows that I loved to sing for Daniel and she invited me along tonight to perform the beautiful song "Perfect Moment". I could sense Daniel's presence all around me the feeling was so strong.

As the music began, I knew I had to do this. I sang the first few lines and my confidence grew, the strength I felt was amazing. At the end Nicola joined me on stage, even her dad got up to sing. The reception I received from the Albert Hotel regulars was so positive that I know I will be singing for them again.

Monday 1st November 2004

I'm back at the Blue Water Studio. Apart from a new engineer named Andy everyone remembered me. Andy was good at his job, he relaxed me and I felt confident. The recording went well and I was asked to be there on Wednesday for a check on all ten tracks and also to agree label designs for my album.

Wednesday 3rd November 2004

The labels were ready; there was a butterfly on the front and a moth for the back, pictures Andy had taken. Once things had been checked and agreed Andy began to press copies of the CD and print the labels. The title I chose was "Moving On". This was just another way to demonstrate how my life has turned round since making my first album a year ago, titled "Life Goes On".

The first CD to come off the production line went into a padded envelope and I sent it to my singing partner. I felt a bit sad, he had recorded two of the songs with me as a duet yet his name wasn't on the CD, but it was his choice not to be named on the label.

Friday 5th November 2004

I received a text message from my singing partner saying he had received the CD and thought it was "wicked". I am so happy that he likes it but just to make sure I am going to send him a text tomorrow asking for an honest opinion of our songs.

Saturday 6th November 2004

Tim replied to my text saying that he loved the duets, which was good enough for me. I am now satisfied the album is alright. Today I took the albums to Pendulum Records. The owner said he would put them on the shelves right away. Another goal had been achieved.

Wednesday10th November 2004

Unable to sleep I went downstairs to make a mug of tea. In the quiet of the early hours it's surprising how the mind wanders. At some stage in her teens my mother (Gillian) gave birth to an illegitimate daughter named Marilyn. I found myself thinking about her.

Through a bit of detective work I have already discovered she gave birth in Liverpool and that her family disowned her. Having a child out of wedlock in those days was akin to a mortal sin. My mother was banished from the family home and that was how she and Marilyn finished up living in a guesthouse somewhere in the Retford area. Soon after arriving in Retford she met and married my father. Marilyn lived with them until my mother found herself pregnant again, at which time she decided to have Marilyn adopted. Marilyn would have been three and a half years old so the adoption took place sometime in the early 1950's.

The Salvation Army sorted out the arrangements and Marilyn was put on a train at Retford railway station from where she would travel on her own to Durham. Here a doctor and his wife, who would become her adopted parents, met the train. Although my father was not in agreement with what my mother was doing, she knew best as always. My mother did discuss this part of her life with us when we were old enough but never once did she show any regret for her actions. Somewhere out there I have a half sister who I would like to trace yet perhaps it may be best to leave well alone.

Monday 15th November 2004

At around 9.30 pm I had an impulse to telephone Simon's (my son) foster mother. I'm pleased that I did, as she told me that Simon had bought my book, the content had shocked him and he'd thrown it away in anger. He had been shielded from my past and reading the book had made him ill. I felt really bad about it. Why is it that even though I love my children I still hurt them?

Wednesday 17th November 2004

Feeling confused and guilty about Simon I decided to phone Michael. Sandra answered the phone and listened to my problem. When I had finished telling her about Simon's reaction to my book she said that he would eventually come back to me. Because of the confusing things that have happened in his life, Sandra said that he needed to sort things out in his mind.

Thursday 18th November 2004.

I awoke feeling different, refreshed, as if something had changed, but I had no idea what.

Later, whilst out shopping, I bought a card for Simon. On the front it said "we can make it", with a beautiful verse both inside and out. I decided I had to do something to make the first move.

I went to see Clair and met Michael coming out of her shop. I told him what had happened and he was sure that Simon would come back and so was Clair when I told her too. However hard they tried to convince me I am still not sure that we can make it up.

I went home and mulled over in my mind what I would write inside the card, the verses said it all but I still needed to write something. I know that he doesn't call me mum, just Rosie, so I listened to what my heart was telling me. I asked him if he would mind reading the words in the card. I wrote that I was the one who was sorry and signed it from Rosie and I added both my telephone numbers to the message hoping he would call me.

I have no idea what will become of my attempt to make amends, I was in the wrong all those years ago, I should not have tried to make him apologise for helping me when I had the seizure. The fit had loosened my hold on reality and I was unaware that he was just trying to help me. Losing my temper must have hurt him; after all he was only doing what he thought best for me at the time.

Friday 19th November 2004

My phone rang late afternoon - it was Simon. If it is possible for anyone to go into total shock I did. I was not sure what to say but managed "hello love, are you alright?" His reply was straight to the point. He told me not to send any more cards and to stop leaving messages with his foster mother. He wanted nothing to do with me or to know about my past, all of which had happened before he was born. He made it clear that I was to stay out of his life. He was moving on and that was that.

He spoke quickly, not stopping to draw breath. It was as if he was reading from a prepared script. When he had finished I replied, "Well, at least I know how you feel," and the conversation ended.

I felt physical pain, as if I'd been kicked in the stomach. It was like losing Daniel all over again, only in a different way. Still holding the telephone I had to call someone, anyone. Why I rang the WPC who had supported me at the time of my court case I'll never know but that is what I did. She listened as I blurted everything out, I could not control my emotions, the hurt inside me was unbearable. When I finally let her get a word in I didn't really listen but I remember her saying that she would come to see me tomorrow.

Saturday 20th November 2004

I didn't sleep much last night. When I awoke, feeling absolutely rotten, I lay in bed thinking, hoping it had all been a bad dream. Of course I knew it hadn't. It was when I saw my reflection in the mirror that I knew I was in a right state. Maybe Simon had done me a favour. Although I felt as if my heart had been ripped out I realised it was final. The realisation hit me that Simon had been taken from me, he, like Daniel, had gone forever.

Around mid-morning my friend the WPC arrived. Although I knew she could do nothing about my situation, it wasn't a police matter after all, she sat and listened, and with her having children she understood how I was feeling. I think talking it out helped.

In the evening, I went to the spiritualist church and told Michael what had happened. He still told me to give my son time, that he has had a lot to come to terms with. I felt a little better as I have every confidence in what Michael says.

The spiritualist medium began by asking, "who in the room has been feeling really down?" I looked at Michael who nodded his head, so I nervously put my hand up. Although the medium said she might not return to me she asked if I was angry about something? I told her that I was. She said I was very fragile at the moment and I began to cry. As the tears tracked down my face a young woman in the crowd gave me a tissue, and another brought a glass of water.

After the medium had finished speaking to me I told Michael that even though it was my youngest son Simon who she had linked with I could feel Daniel, who is in spirit, down my left side. After she had been to many other people in the crowd the spiritualist returned to me, which was unexpected. She reminded me of how fragile I was, she repeated "gently, gently", many times over. Her voice was soft and calming.

Thursday 2nd December 2004.

Amongst the usual assortment of letters and junk mail in my mail box there was an ominous brown envelope. I'm not keen on brown envelopes at the best of times but this one stopped me dead in my tracks. I was to be visited by officers of the Fraud Investigation Unit. There was no indication as to why they wished to visit me but I had to know so I rang the number on the letterhead. I was told they had received an allegation that I was running a taxi business from my home address and as I was receiving benefit this was a criminal offence. Presumably someone had seen John's taxi coming and going from outside my house and reached the wrong conclusion. Or it could be someone who wished me ill will was engaged in malicious troublemaking.

Whatever the source of this allegation it was entirely false and the man from the Fraud Investigation Unit who I spoke to must have thought I had gone completely mad because in between bouts of raucous laughter I asked him if it was some kind of joke. In a pompous way he assured me that it wasn't and to prepare myself to be investigated. I told him I would look forward to meeting his colleague on the following Monday and put the phone down.

That evening I had an appointment with my doctor. I was in a lot of pain from my neck, shoulders, back and most of my joints too. My doctor thought it was muscular but he used a more complicated name for it. All he could put it down to was that I must have had a seizure causing all my muscles to go into spasm. I'd lost quite a lot of weight as well, which was something he said to keep an eye on. During our conversation he told me that he had purchased my book. I could not believe it to begin with until he mentioned some of the things that were in it. I thanked him, as not many doctors would even take an interest, but he did.

Saturday 4th December 2004

I was at the Spiritualist church when the medium came across to me. She said there was someone in spirit, a gentleman who I adored and she asked if my dad was still here or not. I told her that he had passed away and yes I did adore him. She told me that it was him who was keeping me going, giving me that extra push when I needed it. Sometimes she said that I would feel his hand on my shoulder giving me the strength to carry on and she was right. My dad would never want me to fail or go under.

Sunday 5th December 2004

For some reason I was feeling down today but I couldn't think why. Perhaps the worry of the fraud investigation was getting to me. It was getting closer to Christmas as well and Daniel was on my mind.

Daniel loved Christmas, particularly the tree, which always made him smile. I went up to his bedroom where everything is kept exactly the same as when he was alive. I sat on his bed and looked up at the top of his cupboards where the Christmas decorations and tree are kept and I began talking to him, telling him how I proposed to put the tree and all the trimmings up without him being here. I knew that he would never forgive me if I didn't put them up, as this was the best time of the year for him.

I have always made a feature out of my Christmas tree, with my mother never bothering to have one once dad had died. So I pulled myself together and thought of what might have been and took all the decorations downstairs.

The baubles are made from mouth blown glass and the tinsel and two sets of lights were of the best quality too – nothing but the best for Daniel. As I put it all together I kept looking at Daniel's photograph, I knew this was something I had to do for both of us. Two and a half hours later it was finished. I sat back, viewed my handiwork and cried.

John came to see me later on and he commented that I could always make a Christmas tree look great no matter what. We had a meal together, and watched some television. I was really tired but felt that it had been worthwhile.

Monday 6th December 2004

I was in trepidation about the visit from the Fraud Investigation Unit. Even though I had committed no crime it was in my mind that, with my luck, there would always be the possibility that I would not be believed and taken to court.

The day dragged on and no one came so I began to convince myself that nothing was going to happen. Well, nothing did happen except for John receiving a letter later in the week saying that no proceedings would take place. Obviously the fraud people had realised that the allegations were groundless and dropped the case. However, the experience created a tendency for me to look over my shoulder more often, which is sad really.

Christmas Eve 2004

I decided to visit the Moth and Lantern pub at Cottam as I know the man there who runs the karaoke. This evening he'd placed the speakers on the floor. As I began to sing I must have walked in front of one of them causing loud feedback, it was really bad. The man barged me away from the speaker then, in front of everyone, he asked in an aggressive tone if I was trying to blow his gear up. I was that embarrassed I didn't know where to look, but I knew I had to finish the song.

Afterwards, I phoned John who came straight away to collect me. What upset me most was that I have known this man for years and he knew what I had been through with my brother. I felt bullied and humiliated by what he had done. The lights on Daniel's tree cheered me up a bit when I got home but I went straight to bed, I'd really got nothing to stay up for.

Christmas Day 2004

John was joining me so I made an early start on Christmas lunch. He knew that without his company I would spend Christmas alone. John has a sensitive side to him, which I like. By the time he arrived I'd done the housework and prepared all the vegetables and whatever I could do in advance to save time, or maybe just to keep busy and occupied. We enjoyed the day and later on watched a few films on television. He knew I wasn't in a particularly good frame of mind so it was a bit like treading on eggshells for him.

I did try and managed to survive the day without major upset but I had a few tears before he left. I don't think he minded - he seemed to understand why I was upset.

Monday 3rd January 2005

Just prior to Christmas I had visited my dentist because a crack had appeared in my dentures. He told me to super glue them together until a new set could be made. Well, I was not amused when I had to attend the casualty department at my local hospital. The glue had burnt my mouth causing painful swelling. The casualty officer was appalled by what he saw and was quite uncomplimentary about my dentist. Antibiotics and other tablets eventually reduced the swelling but I'd learnt a valuable lesson - gluing dentures with superglue is not a good idea. I just had to take extra care not to damage them further.

Wednesday 12th January 2005

I had a doctor's appointment and I always allow myself plenty of time to get ready wherever I am going. I decided to clean my teeth, which I knew were very fragile. To my horror as soon as I touched them with the toothbrush they snapped in half. What could I do? I only had thirty minutes before my taxi would arrive. I couldn't use superglue again it would kill me. Then it occurred to me what to do. I rarely throw anything away as I am a hoarder.

I went upstairs to my bedroom and foraged through my dressing table drawers where I knew there was a set of dentures from seven years ago. Clothes were scattered everywhere in my panic to find them. Then, to my relief, there they were, sitting in a plastic bag – smiling at me. I went to the bathroom, hoping and praying they would fit. To my surprise they did, perfectly. Who would have thought that after seven years I had kept an old set of dentures? If I'd remembered sooner I could have spared myself the agony caused by the superglue.

Thursday 20th January 2005

I'd been feeling unwell all day so I telephoned the surgery to inquire if they had any vacant appointments. They hadn't but the receptionist told me that if I still felt the same later that evening to call the "out of hours" number. I decided to leave it a little longer but my coughing was getting worse - my rib cage was hurting quite a lot. I rang the number and was told that I had to go to the local hospital, and they would send a car for me. On the way the driver was quite amiable, trying to engage me in conversation but I didn't feel much like talking. At the hospital I was given antibiotics then began the return journey home. I never thought that an innocent conversation with a hospital car driver would put me in a situation where I felt uncomfortable. On arriving home, the driver gave me his telephone number. He also told me what his hours of work were. He asked me to go out with him. I told him I would think about it.

Friday 21st January 2005

The following morning there was a knock at my back door. It was the driver from the hospital car service; he was holding a card and a large bunch of flowers. Not wishing to be rude I invited him into the kitchen where he told me that he was going to telephone but decided just to come round. I said there was no need for him to have brought me flowers and his presence made me feel quite uneasy.

He commented on what a nice home I had then asked to use the bathroom. I felt that he was being too familiar. Returning from the bathroom he asked quite openly what I was doing the following day. He suggested that he either came to my home or we could go for a drive. By now I was regretting ever having let him inside the house. He was so persistent it made my skin crawl. I had to tell him that I was not interested but I suppose fear got the better of me, as I had no idea of this man's background. I made some excuse about having an appointment and he left but not before writing down his mobile phone number.

Later on I sent him a text message explaining that I could not get involved and I would sooner be by myself. I don't know how he took this but not long afterwards someone rang my mobile phone anonymously. It was probably the persistent driver. To my relief it didn't happen again and I haven't heard from him since.

Saturday 22nd January 2005

In the evening I went to the Spiritualist church and told Michael what had happened. He suggested that I reported the driver to the hospital, as he may try to do this again with other women. I knew that he was right, yet I could not do it. This man had left me feeling afraid.

If I reported this incident it would result in him losing his job so, being scared of repercussions, I let it go. I told John about it and he said things like that should not be allowed to happen but he knew how much it had scared me and understood why I could not report it.

I hadn't realised the full extent of what this had done to me until a day or so later I was watching television when there was a power cut. My house was plunged into darkness and I was convinced my unwelcome admirer had returned, so I panicked. The house phone, being powered from the mains, had gone off, so in the dark I stumbled around trying to find my mobile to contact John. The light from my mobile phone gave some relief and John said it was most likely a general power cut and that I should look through my window to see if my neighbour's lights were off. They were, which made me feel a bit of an idiot, but you never know if someone is harbouring a grudge, they will resort to anything.

Friday 4th February 2005

Today was the 36th anniversary of my father's death. I looked across at the large picture that I have of him on my bedroom wall and told him that I didn't blame him for dying and leaving me at the mercy of my mother and brother. There are some people who would blame a parent who had passed away if they were hurt as much as I was. It was only after he had died that I discovered how much he had protected me. His death may have been 36 years ago but he will always be my very special dad.

Friday 18ᵗʰ February 2005

Nicola called round to see me. Her baby is due in a few weeks and I thought how well she looked. We chatted and I showed her my photograph album in which I kept the newspaper clippings and photographs taken during my book signing. She read my book review from Victim Support and thought it was wonderful. I made it clear that as soon as she went into labour someone was to call me. We laughed about it and she told me that she had already listed the people who were to be told. Nicola will make an excellent mother as she comes from a wonderful family and is a friend who cares.

Saturday 19ᵗʰ February 2005

This evening I went to the Spiritualist Church. There were no messages for me from the medium but in the circle, which we have afterwards, I was told someone was "bugging me". I knew who it could be. He advised me to get off my backside and get something done. I replied that I intended to and was overcome when someone told me that I was going to be a nurse, I told her that I had always wanted to be and she was convinced that I would be. Who knows what lies ahead for any of us? Perhaps there was a link here with Nicola's baby.

Friday 4th March 2005

Nicola told me yesterday that she was being admitted to hospital today. The birth of her baby was to be induced. All day I waited for a call to say that she had given birth, but there was nothing.

I decided to go out in the evening but left my mobile switched on just in case. Previously, I had met up with one of my cousins and her partner, and have been sitting with them each week for about a month. It's been good catching up on things. From her comments I think she was a bit like I was at home, pretty much the black sheep of the family.

Once again, I chose to sing "Over The Rainbow". At the end I felt sadness, perhaps it had something to do with Mothers' Day being so close.

Saturday 5th March 2005

I was beginning to worry about Nicola and her baby so I telephoned the maternity ward. I explained to the nurse who I was as I knew that Nicola did not want the baby's father to know anything. The nurse passed the phone to Nicola; I was as excited as she was. I bombarded her with questions. She told me she had had a daughter at 8 am that morning, and she weighed in at 6 lbs 10 ozs. I was so proud of her, it was her first baby and she had experienced a long labour, which meant she needed to rest. I asked her to let me know when she was out of hospital and to give her baby a cuddle from me when she woke up. I was so pleased that the nurse did that for me.

Sunday 6th March 2005 - Mothers' Day.

The last gift I remember receiving was from Daniel a few months before he died. Although I have four other children, I would not be receiving anything from them this or any other year. It's sad and breaks my heart at times.

Tuesday 8th March 2005

It turned out that Nicola stayed in hospital for two more days. She is so happy and content with her baby. She is a person who is well organised and knows what she wants. I know that I have to give her some space as she will be busy getting a routine together, and all the family will be wanting to visit her too.

CHAPTER FOUR ─────────────

I decided to send a text message to Nicola, asking things like "have you chosen a name for your baby yet?" and "is she good?" I knew that Nicola wouldn't have many problems as she had always been determined that everything would be alright. I was delighted when she sent a reply asking if I would be in that afternoon. Shortly afterwards another text message came from her saying that she would arrive in about 20 minutes. I have to admit my heart was all of a flutter. I didn't want to let her down by getting emotional. As this would have been the first newborn baby I had seen since losing Daniel.

I opened the patio doors to let some fresh air flow through the room. I was a little worried about what the cat's reaction would be, as she had never seen a baby before. At that precise moment, around 12.15 pm, a knock came at my door. I knew it had to be Nicola; I was all fingers and thumbs. On opening the door I was so surprised, there she was stood with her baby daughter in a car seat and they both looked wonderful.

"Don't knock, come in," I told her. Nicola didn't look like she'd had a baby at all. She had lost all her weight and looked great. I couldn't stop looking at the baby, "What's her name?" I asked. Nicola said it was Lucy Jane, it really suited her, she had a gorgeous button nose. I was asking all the questions I could, and then felt myself choking up, I had to pull myself together. I thought it best if I made a drink at this stage. Then I was alright, it was just the initial shock I think, just a few memories being brought back to me. As for the cat, well, she went near Lucy's chair a few times, and Nicola watched every move but there were no problems.

Apart from moving around a little, Lucy slept through the whole visit. It was getting near to Lucy's feeding time so Nicola began to get ready to go home. I could not believe what a perfect mother she is, a natural. When they had left I sat in the quiet just thinking of when my son Daniel was as tiny as Lucy. I still have vivid memories of his childhood; they will stay with me until I die. I am pleased that I held my emotions in check whilst Nicola was here; Lucy is such a treasure, and a credit to her mum.

Tuesday 15th March 2005

I have decided to make a few more changes in my life, so I telephoned the job centre. I receive a disability allowance for having epilepsy and was beginning to get bored of being at home all day doing nothing. I was told that one of their officers would telephone me soon.

Thursday 17th March 2005

I received a telephone call today from the job centre and we had a good chat. I explained how I wanted some kind of employment, and he seemed to understand. I have arranged to meet him at the job centre next Tuesday to find out what help he can give me.

Friday 18th March 2005

Last night as I lay waiting for sleep to overtake me I heard the clock strike 12 o'clock signalling the beginning of a new day, what would have been my father's birthday. When the clock finished chiming I found myself talking to him. I told him all about the bad things that had happened since he had gone, and how much I still loved and missed him, and wished he could still be here. Though I know none of this can bring him back, he is always in my heart.

I went to the Spiritualist Church today, hoping there might be just a slight chance that I would get a message from my dad or Daniel. I sat on the front row next to Michael and I felt so relaxed and was really enjoying the evening. The medium that evening was a lady and she was really good. She walked in my direction and said she was being drawn to someone with an Irish connection. I looked at Michael and he nodded, as my dad was half Irish, so I put my hand up. I noticed another woman had done the same.

The medium said she had the month of March. My dad's birthday was in March, how close could she have got? I was told she didn't want me, as the other woman had taken the message. I began to get angry as she then said she had the month of June, which was the month when Daniel was killed, yet the other woman still took it. I felt like turning around and telling her it wasn't her message. Then the medium said she could hear someone singing Danny Boy. I had had that song played at my son's funeral. I was in pieces.

It wasn't like me to behave as I did but at the interval I went to everyone I knew. When they asked if it was because someone else had taken the message I said it wasn't, but inside I knew it was, I think it's wrong and cruel to do such a thing.

I telephoned John to collect me, and he asked what was wrong. By this time I was near to tears. "Don't let it bother you," he said, but I argued with him all the way home. After he'd dropped me off at home I sent him a barbed text message saying how dare he patronise me, I have always had to fight for everything in my life. He tried calling me, but I hung up.

Later I had a message on my phone from him saying it wasn't his fault. That was true but it was the whole principle of what had happened that was wrong, and I couldn't fight that. I get tired of fighting, life isn't always fair, but I just have to carry on. Everyone still says that

I should stay in touch with the Spiritualist Church. It may all seem petty to some people, but I felt totally deprived that evening, of something that could have meant so much to me.

Saturday 19th March 2005

Last night I went to The Albert Hotel and sat with my cousin and her partner. I sang quite a few songs including two special ones for my dad, "I Believe", and "The Wonder Of You". These were his favourite songs. After singing "I Believe" I told Neil, who runs the Karaoke, that it was for my dad and he announced it over the microphone.

When I arrived home, I sat and told dad of my evening, that I didn't know if he was listening but I had sung two songs for him. I suppose many people would find it difficult to understand why I did that, but when you wish with all your heart that someone was here it seems the natural thing to do. I suppose it was like giving him a birthday present.

Tuesday 22nd March 2005

I had not long finished a conversation with my publisher when my telephone rang. Answering it, I heard the jolly voice of Gina from Victim Support. She asked how things were going. We had a good chat and then she told me the reason she had phoned. She had contacted her training manager who had then contacted the Area executive with a view to my book going "national". I was given the name of a person in the media department. Gina wanted my permission to let him have all my details and my postcode. I readily agreed, who wouldn't? She said it wouldn't happen overnight, but someone may be contacting me. I couldn't thank her enough, and I am just waiting now for that one important telephone call.

Saturday 2ⁿᵈ April 2005

Clair sent a text message; I was speechless when I read it. Clair had agreed to sell my book in her shop and the message was that she had sold 10 copies. I replied to the message saying how pleased I was, and to thank her. I still cannot believe it is still selling seven months after it was published. There are more people interested in my past than I realised.

Sunday 3ʳᵈ April 2005

John visited me. The day went great without a cross word, which I thought was too good to be true. Usually he would stay until around 11 pm, but that evening he said he was going about 8.45 pm. There had to be a reason, I knew John too well. I knew he was lying by the excuses he gave for having to leave early. An argument flared and many harsh words were said. I insisted that we went to his house for the rest of the night; I had to find out what was going on.

After arguing again I smashed a photograph of Daniel on the floor. I also smashed two beautiful ornaments that stood on my marble fireplace. We decided to call a truce and go to his house. On arrival he tried his best to convince me that he had changed, but I knew better. He told me that he was not happy and was feeling really down. John has tried numerous times to make a move on me but I cannot let him near me physically.

John invited me to sit beside him on the sofa to talk. I never saw further than the end of my nose. How stupid could I have been? I felt his arm go around my shoulders and I froze. I am ashamed to say that we had sex. He said we could do this every week, I felt like a whore, which is maybe how he wanted me to feel. On my return home I wished that I had never entered his house, feeling so cheap and dirty. I thought John of all people would have understood what doing something like that could do to me. Or maybe he did, and this was his way of getting back at me for all that has gone wrong between us.

Monday 4th April 2005

I telephoned John asking him to take me to town. When I got in the car I noticed a big smirk across his face that I felt like wiping off. I decided to be strong and ask him if he felt better for the night before, but I wasn't up to questioning him. I called in on Clair at her shop and confided in her what had happened; I don't think she could believe it.

The main reason for going into town was to follow up a job vacancy in a café that I regularly frequented. I left my details and the proprietor said he'd get back to me. But, as usual, as soon as I try to do something positive with my life along comes John to put a dampener on things. All he could talk about was the wages. He couldn't see that I have never been employed because of my epilepsy and that now just might be the right time for me to take a large step forward, but all he did was try to talk me out of it.

Later in the day Nicola with her new baby called to see me. I was amazed at how much Lucy had grown. I was a little disappointed that I never got to hold her, but I suppose there will always be other times.

Wednesday 6th April 2005

I needed some help in my struggle to understand why I had given in to John's advances, so I contacted Gina. She was understanding and sympathetic. Gina explained how my brain works after all those years of being abused by my brother. She said that when I froze and allowed John to have his way it was as if I was with my brother and not allowed to make a noise or say no to him. I am petrified that that feeling will remain with me for the rest of my life.

My conversation with Gina lasted for about 30 minutes then she arranged to visit me at home at the end of the week. During my conversation with Gina, John had been trying to telephone me and couldn't get through. When he finally did it was just like an interrogation. "Who had I been talking to for so long?", "why was it necessary to have such long conversations?". I had to partly lie and say that Gina had contacted me about the talk I was planning and that my publisher had been speaking to me as well. When I asked him why he wanted to know he told me that he thought I'd done something stupid, like call the police. John must have realised how wrong it was to do what he'd done to me. I continued to see him most days but we agreed that he would never touch me physically again. From now on our relationship was one of friendship and no more.

Friday 8ᵗʰ April 2005

Gina had arranged to see me at 2 pm. This would be the first time I'd met her face to face. All I knew about her is that she had a wonderful jolly voice. The day dragged a little to begin with and then, before I knew it, I was preparing myself to meet Gina, the woman who shares all my misfortunes.

It was just after 2 pm when I heard her knock. Nervously I went to the door. I didn't know what to expect, but then again neither did she. I could see straight away that she was no taller than myself. I am less than 5 foot tall. I already had an image of Gina and she looked just as I expected she would. She came in and made herself at home. It was great to chat and laugh. She was everything someone would like in a big sister. Gina stayed for a good couple of hours and then it was time for her to leave. I spoke more openly and felt much more at ease with her than with my own family.

I don't know if Gina had brought me some luck but that night I won £75 at my local public house. I shocked myself and everyone else when I told the girls behind the bar to buy all my friends a drink out of my winnings. To me, winning the money was a bonus, so why not share good fortune.

The following day I received a telephone call from Clair. She'd had a conversation with a customer who had bought my book. The customer, a woman, asked Clair for my telephone number as she said she needed help. It appeared that her past was similar to my own. Clair would not give my telephone number to anyone, but she told the woman that she would pass on her details then leave me to decide whether to make contact. I chose to get in touch to see what kind of help this person needed. I was speaking to her for quite some time, and then arranged to meet her in Clair's shop on the Monday morning.

Monday 11th April 2005

Just before 9 am my phone rang, I wasn't expecting a call from anyone. It was my publisher. He'd been away for a week and was just catching up on things. I mentioned this meeting to him and how I was nervous about it. He gave me his advice, which was to keep a distance between the woman and myself. He said that I should not allow myself to get too involved. I was grateful for this advice and ended the conversation by saying that I would let him know what happened.

When I arrived at Clair's shop the woman was already there. She seemed about the same age as me but taller and heavier. I took her to the café next door, found a corner table and embarked on what turned out to be a lengthy conversation about a wide range of things. I began to have doubts about how I could help her.

She had written several books (she didn't say what about) and was unsure of what to do next, except she wanted to write her autobiography. Well, if I can write one, having never written anything before, she would have a head start. It was then she informed me that her real intention was to set up a printing and publishing company. All the stuff about having a background similar to mine was nothing more than a ruse to pick my brains about the company I wrote for. My publisher's advice was sound; I was pleased that I had kept my distance.

Friday 15th April 2005

In the evening I went to the Albert Hotel. There were only a few customers at the bar so, along with one of my friends, I sang more than my usual number of songs. I enjoy being in the public eye. John was forever telling me to be careful; particularly as the newspaper coverage of my book and CD's may make some people vindictive. Perhaps he'd heard gossip in the taxi. He warned me that my better nature could be taken advantage of. Well, he was right, as I was to learn, that very evening.

One of the men in the Albert Hotel, who I thought I knew quite well, was being his usual friendly self, or so I thought. There were a few of us stood around the bar and when my taxi arrived he still had a full pint of beer left. I said goodbye to my friend and a few others. It was then I noticed that he'd consumed the whole pint in one go. He'd told me earlier that he lived on the same street as myself, which I had doubts about. He offered me a lift home. I said an emphatic "no". Getting into a car with someone I didn't know anything about, apart from the fact that he'd been married for 30 years, would be asking for trouble. He asked if he could walk me outside to my taxi. I couldn't see the harm in it but once we were at the door he said people would talk. My reputation was good and I had every intention of keeping it that way.

Outside, my taxi was waiting opposite the Albert Hotel, yet he still kept insisting that I get in his car. When I refused he asked if he could visit me sometime. I was so harassed and wanting to get away from him I foolishly agreed, but didn't tell him my address. I told the taxi driver what had happened and in his rear view mirror he could see the man following us. He was trying to find out where I lived. Once inside I locked the doors then phoned the taxi driver on his mobile.

He told me that the man had cruised by my house to see which one it was. Usually, I will telephone John or send him a text letting him know that I am alright, but that night I didn't. I was so ashamed at how stupid I had been.

Then my phone rang. It was John, asking me why I had not called him. I told him what had happened. He was not happy with me particularly as he had repeatedly warned me that some men might think of me as an easy target after what happened with my brother. For the rest of the weekend I never went out. My doors were locked and bolted; I was petrified that the man might come back. I learned a valuable lesson that night.

Once the fear had subsided I felt angry that I had allowed myself to feel pressurised and intimidated. No woman should have to put up with that.

Sunday 17th April 2005

I awoke feeling quite low. Apart from my experience with the man from the Albert Hotel there was another reason why I should be feeling as I did. Today was my brother's birthday and my eldest daughter Samantha's too. I could feel all the hate running through me.

Doing the housework is usually therapeutic but not today. I seemed to take my anger out on everything. The vacuum cleaner became a guided missile. I aimed it at everything except Alfie my cat. The bitterness inside me grew until I felt like screaming then, gradually, it subsided. John visited me at lunchtime. He wanted to check how my talk at Worksop library on Tuesday evening was coming along. To begin with he didn't want anything to do with it, but he realised now how much it meant to me.

Monday 18th April 2005

It was teatime when the telephone rang. John was calling to tell me that details of my talk had been on the local radio. The announcer gave details of the venue, time and what the talk was about. I think this shocked John a little because now he knew I wasn't making it all up, it was actually real. To my relief he offered to drive me to Worksop.

Tuesday 19th April 2005

My big day, the talk about my book would take place this evening. Throughout the day I took everything in my stride to save energy for what I knew would be a nerve racking experience. On arrival at Worksop Library the butterflies in my stomach had grown in size – they felt more like albatrosses. Then, almost in an instant, I felt good about the whole thing. I don't know what took all the fear and worry away from me but I felt strong inside, I was ready to face anything.

The audience settled and my publisher introduced me. He said supportive things about my book and myself and then it was my turn. I began by thanking everyone for coming and then the words just seemed to flow. When I came to explain about taking a break from writing because of Daniel's death I found previously unanswered questions pouring into my mind. These questions were about what I should have asked the police at the time of Daniel's accident. Why couldn't the driver remember going diagonally across a straight road to collide with a telegraph pole? Were the driver and my son having an argument? Were they messing around with the radio? For the driver to say in a court that he couldn't remember was no kind of answer. He'd only passed his driving test three days prior to the accident and yet he was not ordered to retake his driving test. I think the law would be different if I had stabbed someone and then pleaded loss of memory. I'd be laughed out of court.

The only person who knows what happened that day is the driver but I don't think he will ever come forward with the truth, which means there will never be any real closure for me.

Although most of my talk was quite sad, I decided to say something at the end that would lighten things up a bit. I told my audience about my two daughters in Scotland, how their adoption was an open one. I explained that I was still in touch with their adoptive mother by telephone and that they refer to her as mum and to me as their England mum. I explained that I receive regular photographs of them so I am able to watch them grow up. This was the happy ending my audience needed as faces broke into smiles and their applause was genuine.

Some of the people remarked how natural and professional I had sounded. This was even more remarkable because I hadn't even rehearsed it. David, the security man made me laugh when he told me that he was trying to read his newspaper but all he could do was listen to me talking.

Afterwards I felt proud, as if I had achieved something very special. My publisher praised me and told me that my talk was 'spot on', so I knew that he was happy.

Before leaving I had a cup of tea and a chat with my audience then a lady who lives in my hometown brought me back. I asked her if she could take me to John's house, as he would want to know how I had got on. He could tell by my face that I was overjoyed and when I sat down and told him all about it he even listened, which I must say was good for John.

The following morning, I sent a text message to Clair telling her all about the talk. Even though I had already told John, I was just bursting with joy that I needed to tell someone else. Then I made a call to Gina at Victim Support and told her. She was so happy for me, saying that she had been thinking of me. It's strange how such a small thing like that can make someone feel good, I suppose that's because I don't take anything in life for granted.

Friday 22nd April 2005

Today I found myself raising even more questions about Daniel's death. Had the police really taken it seriously, or was it just another road casualty among many others they had to deal with? I knew at the time that someone had called for an ambulance, but until I began to search through the newspaper reports of his accident, I was not aware of any witnesses. A man who called for the ambulance saw the accident happen, which he described as unreal.

I couldn't let it rest so I telephoned the Road Traffic Police who dealt with the case. On asking to speak to the officers who had been in charge of the investigation, one being a family liaison officer, I was quizzed as to why it was necessary. I mentioned re-opening Daniel's case but I could tell by the tone of voice of whoever was taking my details that he did not like what I was asking. I was told that someone would be in touch, but after leaving two different messages for two officers, one who is now an Inspector, nobody has yet contacted me.

I remember at the time of Daniel's death how let down I felt but now I am unsure whether the police were ever really interested at all. I have spoken to numerous friends who have all suggested that I should try to re-open Daniel's case. Although I think there is good enough reason for doing so I am scared that raking over the details again would do more harm than good.

CHAPTER FIVE ————————————

Tuesday 26th April 2005

I hadn't been to the Spiritualist church for some time so I phoned Michael. He said I should go back. I suppose there are times when a mother needs answers and I usually got mine through a medium. Later in the day Gina phoned. She had something relevant to discuss with me. Gina had been given a brochure about abuse and felt that it would be a good place to advertise my book. I thanked her then mentioned what I had been trying to do about Daniel's case. She advised me to leave it alone as it could set me back. She reminded me of how far I had come since the accident and that it would be a tragedy to destroy all that progress. She knew I couldn't put it out of my mind completely but said I should try not to let it dominate my life.

In the evening John came to my house. He sat quietly watching television so I picked up my book and began to read it. I knew he had a copy but had not read it. I asked if I could read the preface out loud to him but he told me he would prefer to read it in his own time. I knew that he never would, as he is in denial of the truth and what really happened to me. I knew that I couldn't force him to do something against his wishes but I felt that if he would read it then maybe he would understand the reasons why, at times, I act the way I do.

The following day I woke feeling quite ill. I knew that I should go to see the doctor but I'd possibly get the same answer as the last time I saw him. On that occasion I was told he could not help me unless I stopped smoking so I didn't go. At about 12.45 pm I began to feel really down and then my telephone rang. It was John.

"I've got a message from Jerry," he said.

"Jerry who," I replied.

"Just listen."

John had stopped in his taxi; the song "You'll Never Walk Alone" on, by Jerry and the Pacemakers was playing in his CD player. John knows it was one of my dad's favourite songs. Well, the tears just came from nowhere, I told him you'll have me crying in a minute, though he didn't know I already was. John is like that, people don't understand him, but I do. He doesn't show his feelings, as he is afraid of being hurt, yet he will do things like that and they mean just so much to me. It's not only God who moves in mysterious ways, some people do as well. I have learnt that over the years, but

John is someone I cannot ever compare with anyone else. I suppose after all that has happened between the two of us it must still be that thing called love and no matter how I try it doesn't want to go away.

Thursday 28th April 2005

John visited me and he gave me money for some new clothes that I had seen. He did this just to cheer me up. The following morning I went into Retford where there was a shop that had the most beautiful expensive clothes. I'd been window-shopping there before but never went in. It felt a bit like when I was a kid at Christmas with my nose pressed against the toyshop window looking at a doll my parents could not afford. But now it was different, the money John had given me would let me walk into the shop as a proper customer.

Normally, I don't try clothes on but knowing how expensive they were I wasn't going to take any chances with these purchases. The shop assistant was very helpful and I eventually chose two items, a blue top, which I had drooled over for weeks, and a light lilac one covered in sequins. I felt really good walking out of that shop carrying an elegant bag containing my new clothes. The shop's name on the side of the bag did my "street credibility" a power of good. Everyone could see that it was designer wear.

Before going to the shop I had called in to see Clair to ask what she thought might suit me. A few suggestions were made and when she saw what I eventually bought she said it was a great choice, which made me feel more confident. Then, when John took me home. I showed him and he could see that his money had been well spent.

Saturday 30ᵗʰ April 2005.

I went back to the Spiritualist Church and the medium was so comical, I couldn't stop laughing. He came to me and told me that I had been dragged through hedges backwards and trampled on all of my life and the weight that I had to carry on my shoulders was unreal. However, he said that I was now moving on with my life and trying my best to socialise. He told me that someone in "spirit" was giving me a red brooch to wear on my jacket for love. However, when he said that someone in "spirit" was thanking me for being there the only person that I could think of was Daniel.

I must admit that he certainly knew what he was talking about, as afterwards I went to speak to him. I told him he was correct in all he'd said. I also mentioned my book and he asked me outright if it was abuse that I had suffered. I could not believe his knowledge was so good. It was a great night. I really enjoyed it.

Monday 2ⁿᵈ May 2005 (Bank Holiday)

John doesn't have any holidays at work so he has every Bank Holiday off instead. That evening we went to the Albert Hotel. It was a really good evening, I must have sung about 5 songs and got the crowd singing. Then John sang a favourite song of his and he had them singing too. We played a game called "play your cards right" based on the one hosted by Bruce Forsyth on television. Well, when my ticket was drawn out of the box, I was speechless. I had only won it a few weeks previously. I could hear some people commenting in the background but I didn't care, it is all fair and above board.

I was nervous as John was watching. I chose my 8 cards and began to play. The crowd tried to influence me which cards I should play but I just used my own instinct as to whether the cards would be higher or lower. My next to last card was an ace - I could only go lower. Closing my eyes I put my head down and everyone cheered as I had won again. I bought quite a few drinks for my friends just as I did the last time I won it.

As for John, he looked really pleased and proud of me I suppose, as he'd never seen me do anything like that before. One comment that he did make was "I'm sure that Daniel is with you wherever you go". That meant an awful lot to me, to hear him say something like that. John had put some money towards the tickets so I wanted to share the £100 with him, but he refused. Over the past few weeks I'd seen a side to John that I never knew existed. I told myself that people do change.

Thursday 5th May 2005

This was to be one of those days where a routine visit to the doctor turned into a nightmare. I'd made an appointment to have my three monthly contraceptive injection and whilst I was in the surgery I asked the practice nurse if she could check my left breast as I had felt some lumps in it. She and a colleague checked it and felt the lumps. As a result of this examination I was referred to the Bassetlaw Hospital at Worksop. I was not pleased but I did ask for their help and to get a more thorough check would put my mind at ease.

I think it was more shock than anything that guided me to see Clair and as soon as I told her I just dissolved into tears. She was really good to me and so was Jane, another friend, who was visiting Clare. They both understood my feelings and were very supportive.

The next day I received a telephone call at lunchtime from the Doncaster Royal Infirmary Hospital, with an appointment at the Jasmine Centre for the 16th May at 11.10 am. I was shocked on two counts. I thought I was being seen at Worksop not Doncaster and I had only been referred the day before.

Saturday 7th May 2005

The postman pushed a brown envelope through the letterbox. I couldn't pick it up and just stood looking at it, as I knew what it would be. Eventually I opened it and, as I thought, it was my hospital appointment and a booklet about breast cancer. My whole body was shaking, what if I had cancer? How would I cope?

That same evening, I went to the Spiritualist Church and the medium came to me. She said that a mother figure was present. I was told by the medium that my mother was saying how proud she was of me. The medium seemed surprised that I didn't seem to care what she was telling me. My mother evidently said that I was a clever girl; these were her exact words she used when I was a small child, when my dad was still alive. The medium explained that my mother was frail towards the end, before she passed away. Yes she was, but I didn't care.

This was the first time my mother had come through in spirit, and maybe the last. An apology for the pain and anguish she and my brother had put me through when she was alive would have been acceptable but this was not forthcoming. Rather than being pleased to hear from my mother again I felt only anger and resentment.

Sunday 8th May 2005

This was a good day. Everything went well, even where John was concerned. He came for lunch and we talked. He didn't mind me complaining about not feeling well and all the "what ifs" about the lumps in my breast. That evening we went to the Albert Hotel but my heart was not in it. I sang a few songs but was happy just to sit with a drink.

Thursday 12th May 2005

I had been asleep on the sofa for a while, as I felt really tired. When I woke, my chest felt different. It is difficult to describe but my breastbone appeared swollen. Gently, I poked around to see if there was anything there that I should be worried about. I wasn't over-reacting, for some unknown reason the bone seemed to be swollen. This raised more concerns regarding what they would find at the hospital. Not long after, John telephoned to see how I was. I told him what I had found but he said not to worry. His tone of voice told me that he knew I was scared.

Friday 13th May 2005

I felt so ill. Whether some of my feelings were psychological I didn't know but I just wanted to get my hospital appointment over and done with. I should have been going out to the Albert Hotel but when it came to late afternoon I knew that I had to cancel my taxi. I was angry with myself as I felt that whatever was wrong with me had begun to control my life. This was the first Friday night that I had not gone out in a long time. So I knew things were getting me down.

Saturday 14th May 2005

This was my night to go to the Spiritualist Church. I had to force myself to get ready and arrived on time. The medium went to a few people in the room before asking if anyone knew someone who had "passed" with cancer. I raised my hand. Once again the medium said she had a mother figure that said that I had changed the colour of my hair and it looked nice. The medium asked if my mother would bake a lot. I replied that she would when the family was younger. She told me that she was a good mother. I retaliated and told her she was when we were young, but not as we were growing up. The medium raised her voice at me and said that I was changing what she had been told. I wasn't going to admit to her being a good mother, which would not be true.

When the medium and many other people had left the church, there remained a circle where some of the people can link to "spirit". One woman, who was a medium, came towards me. She said that my mother was with her. I was told that my mother knew how much I was hurting inside and wished she could turn back the clock. She didn't expect me to forgive her, but to try and move on.

I felt that if this was my mother, then all she was doing was patronising me, which wouldn't get her very far. Nobody knows what hurt and anger I have inside of me, least of all her.

Sunday 15th May 2005

All day I was on edge about visiting the hospital. I tried my best to keep busy and occupied my mind with other things, though it didn't work very well. John came to see me but he knew how upset I was. He stayed with me all day, so I have a lot to thank him for.

That evening, before leaving to go home, he said he would try to call round the following morning. He wanted to make sure I was alright prior to me leaving for Doncaster Royal Infirmary. Once settled into bed, I set my alarm clock for 6.30 am. I knew I had to be ready from 8.30 am onwards.

Monday 16th May 2005

I was awake well before the alarm was set to go off. I really didn't want to go to the hospital, I was petrified of what they would find. John called by in plenty of time to wish me luck. Although he tried to put my mind at ease what he was saying didn't register.

The journey to the hospital seemed to take forever. On arrival I checked in at the reception and waited. As each name was called I felt myself jump. I cannot describe how I felt, numb I suppose - trying to put my brave face on again, but inside my stomach was in knots. Then my name was called. I stood up and followed the nurse. I felt so lost and alone, yet I had come this far so I couldn't turn back. The nurse was gentle and reassuring. Handing me a gown she explained that I should undress from the waist up then put it on.

I did as she asked, but it was when she said she was going to call the doctor into the room that I felt myself begin to panic.

I needn't have worried because the doctor was really nice. He confirmed there was a lump of some description there. He said that I should have a mammogram, which didn't worry me too much as I had been examined in this way before. The nurse showed me where to sit and wait, and again this seemed to take forever.

I was finally called and the radiographer who carried out the mammogram seemed to treat me roughly - pushing and pulling my body to achieve the correct position, I understood she had her job to do, but I was very tender and sore, which made the whole thing quite unpleasant.

Once it was over, I was told to go and sit in the waiting area again. I thought I would get my results then be allowed home, but it wasn't as simple as that. Another nurse called me and told me that I had to have an ultrasound scan. I lay on the bed not knowing what I would be told at the end of it all.

A different doctor came into the room. He was very professional looking and asked me where the lump was. I pointed to it. He didn't have much to say, apart from "well done", and left the room. Once again I found myself in the waiting area.

I began to worry. Time was passing and I was the only patient left. Fifteen minutes or so went by then a nurse told me the doctor would like to see me. I felt inside that something was wrong. She showed me into a room where I sat waiting for some time before the doctor came in followed by a different nurse holding a disposable dish with something inside it in her hand.

The doctor explained to me that they needed some cells from the tumour. The lump had now become a tumour and no one had told me. I was now well and truly into panic mode. Things weren't looking good. I asked why the other tests hadn't shown up everything they needed. The doctor said it was to put my mind at ease. I tried different ways of getting information from him, such as what if I don't have it done? He said he couldn't force me but said it was for the best. Inside I knew that I had no choice.

I had the biopsy and was told it would be sent to the laboratory. I was to make an appointment for a week's time. I sent Clair a text message telling her what I'd had done and then rang John. He kept insisting that I shouldn't worry. It was the only way he knew of trying to comfort me. It just seemed as if I was being punished for something and I couldn't understand why all of this was happening to me now.

When I arrived back home, I went straight to see Clair. I was describing everything to her step by step and without warning the tears began to fall. I couldn't keep it in any longer. Clair was wonderful, she made me a drink, and let me sit down, she even offered to go with me for my results next week, but she had already done enough for me. I just hope I can repay her in some way in the future.

Wednesday 18th May 2005

Today I went into town to buy birthday cards and choose a present for Clair. I bought her a silver and purple crystal necklace and a wind chime, which had the verse of "Being a Friend" on it. What I hadn't realised was how draining my hospital experience had been. By the time I arrived home all I wanted to do was sleep. I must have been asleep for well over an hour when the telephone rang. It was John, asking how I was, he knew things weren't right with me; he said that I had lost my spark. In all honesty, I had to agree with him.

Thursday 19th May 2005

I am feeling worse today. I have to keep moving or I won't want to do anything. So I went shopping. I called in to see Clair at her shop and Jane, another friend, came in. They wanted to be with me on Monday when I return back to the hospital for my results, but I declined their offer as Clair had done enough for me already. I knew that if the doctors told me something I didn't want to hear I would probably lose control of my emotions and I wouldn't want my friends to see me like that. Up to this point I had been brave but Monday would be different.

I arrived home with my shopping and the driver wished me luck. Just unpacking my shopping made me out of breath, my chest wall was hurting. As I sat down the phone rang.

"You're back then," it was John, checking how I was. I think it upset him to hear me gasping down the phone. We finished the conversation and I fell into a deep sleep. I woke over an hour later. It was as if I had to keep recharging my batteries. Monday seems a lifetime away, but I need to know why all this is happening to me.

Friday 20th May 2005

Today I sent Clair a text message. I hoped she hadn't been offended by me wanting to go to the hospital alone. She phoned to say that she was not offended and wished me luck. I said I'd phone her from the hospital. I was a wreck, all I wanted to do was lay on the sofa and sleep.

Later, I spent some time on the Internet trying to find out what was wrong with me but deep down I knew it was a futile exercise. I would have to wait until Monday.

I decided to call an old friend. We talked, and she knew straight away something was wrong. She had read my book and remembered the time when I went blind because she saw me wearing a blindfold. She recalled when my meals were put on the floor for me to find. At the time she thought, because my family had told her we were playing blind man's buff, that it was a game. She even remembered my mother kicking the plate to give me some idea of where to find it. That would be my mother's way of covering her tracks, so people wouldn't get suspicious. In reality I had to crawl around the floor, finding my food like a dog, or I didn't eat.

My friend asked why I hadn't told her the true story. This was never an option because my mother would have found out and the consequences would have been awful.

CHAPTER SIX ────────────────

Saturday 21st May 2005.

I awoke early, around 5.40 am, and knew that something was seriously wrong. I found I could hardly move the mid-half of my body. The severity of the pain in my chest was like the pains I remembered when I was younger, when my brother broke my ribs. I was scared, my rib cage was swollen but once out of bed I tried to carry on with normal everyday things.

Later, John came to see me. When I described to him what and how I was feeling he said it was maybe stress, waiting for my hospital results. I was angry; I knew my own body and how it behaves. I waited for him to leave and then telephoned the "out of hours" doctor, I wasn't going to ignore whatever was wrong. I described my symptoms and a lady doctor said that I must be seen. Transport was arranged and when I arrived at the "out of hours" surgery it was my own doctor who saw me. I was so relieved that it was not a stranger.

He examined me and told me I had pleurisy. I'd heard of it but had no real idea what it was. My doctor explained the disease in a straightforward way, then prescribed antibiotics and painkillers. Later, I looked up "pleurisy" on the computer. I discovered that antibiotics are only given if pneumonia is the underlying cause, which frightened me, but at least I am alright. I tried to rest as much as I could for that evening. I cancelled my visit to the Spiritualist church, which was not like me.

Monday 23rd May 2005.

Thank God, I don't have cancer. I need to have regular checks to keep things under control, but that's a small price to pay. When I returned from the hospital I called in to see Clair and immediately burst into tears. They were tears of relief – I wasn't going to die. Clare had bought some flowers for me. Before I received my results Clare had said I would be fine as she could feel nothing bad. How right she was.

Wednesday 25th May 2005

It's John's birthday today, but he was in a really bad mood, I've no idea why. I gave him his presents hoping these would cheer him up. He liked what I'd bought yet his mood stayed sullen. Because I was still suffering with my chest complaint I asked him if he would carry the vacuum cleaner upstairs and run it over the bathroom carpet. Reluctantly, he agreed but when he came back downstairs his mood had worsened so I told him to go to work, I wasn't about to get into an argument.

After he'd left the house I went to look at the bathroom, it hadn't been touched. I was so angry that I dragged the vacuum cleaner upstairs myself. I was in agony but it had to be done. It occurred to me that perhaps John's concern for me was not as genuine as I first thought.

The following morning I had to go to town, it seemed to take ages to get ready, I just was not well enough but struggled around town with my brave face on. I had done the wrong thing. Instead I should have been resting, not going in and out of shops. By that evening I was feeling really weak and knew then that I needed to see the doctor again. That night I hardly slept because of the pain, but I suppose it was the way I was brought up, not to sit around or rest even if you are ill.

Friday 27th May 2005

I practically had to roll out of bed because of the pain in my back. I was so weak, yet I had been eating, and taken my tablets as I was told to. I telephoned the doctor's surgery and was told to go later that morning. Following a long examination my doctor told me he was sending me for a chest x-ray. I was a little concerned because he had written "urgent" on the request form. I went to my local hospital as soon as I could. My doctor had given me an appointment to return to the surgery for the diagnosis.

That evening John called to see me, which was unusual because Friday is one of his busiest days. I knew from the look on his face that something was wrong. He made a drink and then told me why he wanted to see me. His son was visiting again this weekend, yet John had assured me that things would be OK. I told him I wanted no part of it. John's son is using him, only he is too blind to see it, or he doesn't want to see it. I told John that I wanted the rest of his belongings out of the house by the following morning or I would be putting them outside myself.

After he left I phoned Michael, my spiritualist friend who always said John was taking advantage of me. After this I have no doubts that he was right. Following a hard think I sent John a text message asking him to phone me. I explained that I wasn't against his son but I didn't want John to get hurt, as I had been by my youngest son Simon. I just didn't want the job of having to say, "I told you so".

Saturday 28th May 2005.

I got up early and put my face on as usual. I was determined to be my normal self for when John and his son arrived. Yet, when they came in, things seemed different, I don't know why, but all my fears and doubts had left me. I shouted "hello" from the kitchen and went to greet them.

I knew that John had planned for them both to do some gardening, then we were going out for lunch. During the drive to the restaurant, John's son received a call on his mobile – it was his girlfriend. She was enquiring where he was. He told her that he was with his Dad and Mum going to get something to eat. This amazed me and I must admit it caught me unawares. It brought back images of Daniel, as I know he would have said the same thing in the same way, it was uncanny. I felt humbled with it coming from someone so young. It was then that I accepted that he would not hurt his dad in anyway.

That evening, we all went to the Albert Hotel but there was no karaoke, it was a disco. However, it was still good, as we knew the guy who was doing it. Half way into the evening Jackie and Russ came in. I hadn't seen Russ since Christmas Eve, since when I'd been avoiding him. There had been some trouble at the Albert Hotel where we were out doing karaoke and I'd left in a hurry. I was already upset about it being Christmas and Daniel not being there, then something else made me angry so I just left without even saying goodnight. On the night someone had told Russ why I'd left so he held no resentment towards me. It was great to see them again, they met John's son and the night went well.

Bank Holiday Monday 2005

John's son was still here, so I said I would cook lunch. He has his dad's taste where food is concerned. Several times he remarked on how good the food was, he even asked if I'd considered opening my own café. I said that John and me had talked about it many times but I wasn't quite ready to take on the world just yet.

That night we went to the Albert Hotel and I arranged with the landlady to do the catering for my birthday in July. For some reason I was glowing all over, I was so happy. Everyone was listening to John's son singing along to rap music on the karaoke. Then the girl from behind the bar got up to sing, she was the landlord's daughter. We all had a great time. I sang "When a Child is Born", a song that means a lot to me. It's a Christmas song but I love singing it as it reminds me so much of Daniel.

At the end of May 2005 I was not expecting anything particular in the post, but when I checked I found a package marked "photo's - do not bend". Where it had come from I had no idea until I read the postmark. The package was from Glasgow. My friend had sent photographs of my two daughters that she had adopted. Oh, how happy I was, and proud too. They looked so beautiful. The eldest one was wearing a gorgeous white dress with a bright red train down the back, a tiara showing off her long hair. The youngest one was dressed just as smartly; she has beautiful long hair too. She has my features, whereas her sister is the image of her dad. My friend put a note in with the pictures saying she would always thank me for leaving the girls in her care.

I never thought I could make someone so happy, yet inside I felt only sadness. It was my choice to leave them behind, yet my heart ached for them. I suppose that is the price a mother must pay if she wants the best for her children.

Wednesday 1ˢᵗ June 2005.

I would normally be shopping but today I had a doctor's appointment to discuss my x-ray results. Thankfully, there was nothing to worry about. I rushed around town to get all my usual things done then went home. It was only then I realised just how weak I'd become. I put the shopping away, lay on the sofa to rest and fell into a deep sleep. I awoke the following morning at 5.20 am. I'd slept through the afternoon, the evening and through the night. I hadn't eaten or taken my medication. Thinking that I was dreaming I hurried to the bedroom, but I had not slept in my bed at all. I hadn't even taken my make-up off, which was not like me. So, getting my priorities right, I cleaned off my old make-up, washed and styled my hair as I would each morning, then put on a fresh face.

It was when I discovered that my back door had been unlocked all night I realised that John had not called, which is something he normally does. So I must have slept for all those hours, as he would have woken me. This made me angry and I was ready to give John a "piece of my mind" when next I saw him.

I tried to telephone him a couple of times but as he didn't answer I assumed he was getting ready for work. I knew he would get in touch eventually, but I felt confused and my thoughts were woolly. I hadn't just slept heavily but had had an epileptic seizure and that scared me. Eventually, John phoned and immediately I began to get angry but he calmed me down, he knows how the epilepsy controls me.

Then reality hit me. As far as I was concerned when I answered his call it was the following day. When I asked him if he was coming round to see me John didn't seem to know what I was talking about. I had fallen asleep during which time I had suffered a seizure. It was 5.20 in the afternoon when I finally came round, not as I thought, 5.20 in the morning. John explained what had happened and I looked outside, dusk was beginning to fall.

The type of Epilepsy that I have makes my brain act and think differently, and there have been times when I literally thought that I was going mad. In these situations John has always reassured me. Later, I telephoned him and apologised for getting angry. Why he puts up with me I'll never know but he is the sort of man who will help anyone who genuinely needs it. That evening John called to see me and I just burst into tears and held him tightly. I was so frightened at what I had experienced. It all seemed to be so real. John kissed the top of my head and this calmed me. He told me not to worry as stress makes the epilepsy worse. When he had gone I went to bed. I lay there in the dark wondering why things were going wrong again. Maybe it was all the worry from the medical tests. I don't suppose I will ever know.

The next morning I had a phone message from Clair. She was thanking me for her birthday presents. She sounded so excited, as her husband had planned for them to go to Amsterdam on the Monday morning. I was pleased for her, as she really deserved it.

That evening, as usual, I went to the Spiritualist church. It always seems to be my luck that someone tries it on, being sarcastic about my situation. I should have learnt by now not to let things like that get to me but my hackles still rise and when John picks me up he has to spend time reassuring me and telling me to take no notice. I know he is right but for some reason I always rise to the bait.

Wednesday 8th June 2005

Today would have been my mother's birthday. Strangely enough, I didn't feel anything. No sadness, or any kind of emotion. Someone even asked if I had planned to take flowers to her grave, I wouldn't waste my money on her; she wasn't worth it when she was alive so why should I bother now she's dead.

Something great happened today though, whether she was looking down on me or not, I have no idea, but after I had turned my hairdryer off I realised that I had two missed calls on my mobile phone. I didn't recognise the number, so I automatically called it. On the other end a young girl told me that it was a television company, I couldn't believe what I was hearing. She asked for my name and mobile number, once I had given them to her, I was told that the person who had called me would phone again.

Not long afterwards, my mobile phone rang; I was pegging out my washing at the time, it was a glorious sunny day. The caller gave his name as Chris from the Trisha Goddard Show on T.V. It was then I remembered having sent a text message to Trisha in response to a request for possible subject material. Chris asked what it was about, and once I had explained about my book and what it was about, he told me that one of their researchers would get in touch. I told my publisher who said that the T.V. company must be interested otherwise I would not have been contacted. He also had some news that surprised and delighted me. Although my book is in the library of my hometown, he'd had a request for it from two other libraries, one in Oxford and one in Dublin. I felt honoured and proud of how far I had come in such a short space of time. I now had to sit and be patient. Sometimes it's difficult to do that, but as the old saying goes, "all good things come to those who wait".

Saturday 11th June 2005

I hadn't planned to go to the Spiritualist church but John talked me into it. I was pleased that he did as the medium said she had a link with my dad. I loved my dad so much and everything she said about him was true. She mentioned my writing, I told her about the book. She said I would write another one. When I mentioned that this was my second book, she said I would complete a third. My spiritualist friend Michael had also told me that I would write three.

Afterwards, I showed the medium a photograph of my dad and the powerful vibes she got from it were quite disturbing. Then I showed her Daniel's photograph. She told me he wouldn't have suffered or known anything about his death in any way. She knew that he loved life and one of his photographs has books behind him. She told me to look at what it was telling me. I couldn't understand but she made the point that he would have wanted me to write books. I was puzzled when she said that dad mentioned France and America. I didn't know where this information fitted in, so I'd have to wait and see.

Sunday 12th June 2005

Just when I think things are going well something always happens to put a dampener on life. Today John and me went to the Albert Hotel and I sang a few songs that seemed to go quite well. Then the man operating the karaoke came over to me and in front of everyone in the room said that I should sing happier songs, as people had remarked that when I sang they felt like slashing their wrists. At the beginning I thought he was joking, but he repeated it 4 or 5 times. John stood open mouthed, not knowing what to say in my defense. I told John I was going to find the landlady and make a complaint about the man's attitude.

The landlady took me into another room, the karaoke man followed us, trying to apologise. I wouldn't hear of it, his remarks had ruined our evening. I felt so humiliated. The landlord joined us and told me that if I chose not to frequent the Albert Hotel anymore it would be like a piece was missing. At the end of the evening I was still visibly upset and the karaoke man asked me if I would sing a song. I should have told him what to do with his songs, but that wasn't my nature. So he called me up to the front and as I began to sing I felt myself shaking. During the first verse I had to keep my eyes closed as I could feel the tears welling up. I found the strength to sing the whole song and people in the room sang with me but I was pleased when the whole thing was over. I suppose it's like falling off a bike, you just have to ignore the abrasions and get back on again.

This experience taught me a lesson. From that time onwards I would plan my karaoke performances. I'd book a song in, then say a few words about the song before performing it. I have often wondered what was really said, who complained and why. This was the first time anyone had said anything negative about my singing or the songs I chose to sing. Perhaps one day the person responsible will have the courage to tell me to my face instead of going behind my back.

Tuesday 14th June 2005

John visited today; he didn't look himself. I can always tell when something is wrong. My birthday was coming up and I'd booked a room at the Albert Hotel. He told me to cancel my birthday party, he gave me an ultimatum, that if I went ahead with it he wouldn't be there. I told him he couldn't do this to me. I asked for an explanation as to why he was doing this. All he said was that he wouldn't go.

Later that day I phoned both Michael and Clair, I told them about John's attitude. They both agreed that he was trying to control me, perhaps he was jealous or he was trying to protect me against further insults, who knows?

In the afternoon, he took me into Retford to order flowers for Daniel's anniversary. I chose a beautiful long spray in a basket. Although it was still a week away, I wanted to give the florist enough time to do a good job. On the way home John asked if I was still going ahead with my party. I told him that I was and he looked disappointed. He repeated that he wasn't going to turn up; it sounded so childish. He said he would see what the atmosphere was like in the Albert Hotel on Friday then he'd think some more about it. I didn't care either way as nobody dominates my life anymore. I left all that behind years ago.

Well, I had a wonderful night. The Albert Hotel was full and when I looked around to see who I knew, who should be there but my doctor. He waved across the room and said "hello", as I did to him. It was a shock seeing him there, why would a doctor want to attend a karaoke night? The karaoke man, who had previously insulted me, was really pleasant, so I decided life's too short to bear a grudge and I was pleasant back to him. Throughout the evening he made a real effort to make things right, he couldn't have done anymore. John seemed happier.

Tuesday 21st June 2005

Tomorrow I will place flowers on Daniel's grave in remembrance of the day he died. I don't know how I'll feel when they are delivered. It was bad enough choosing them, but placing them on his grave is always heartbreaking.

Previously, I have taken them the day before the anniversary, but I thought this year I would be strong and take them on the day. I don't know why I keep punishing myself like this - I suppose all mothers react in different ways. Already my emotions were beginning to get the better of me, but I had to be strong. Even though Daniel is no longer physically here I still wanted him to feel proud of me. I did small jobs around the house to stay occupied. His death was timed at 11.05 pm on the 21st June 2001; so getting to sleep would be difficult: Daniel would be in my mind all night. I would relive the knock on the door, the visit to A&E, seeing his young lifeless body, and the kindness of the staff. Anyone who thinks that it must have become easier after 4 years can think again. The anger, hurt and pain never leave me.

Wednesday 22nd June 2005

The flowers arrived early; they were beautiful. Seeing them brought back memories of when Daniel's funeral flowers were delivered. I took some photographs of them and then arranged for John to take me to the cemetery. Gently, I placed the flowers on the grave then asked John to take more photos.

The taxi office was pushing John to say how long he would be as jobs were mounting up. He was anxious to get on with his work so I must have spent only 5-6 minutes at my son's grave. Was it really worth it?

On arriving home I was so tired I fell asleep. On waking, I immediately apologised to Daniel's photograph, saying how sorry I was that I didn't stay longer at his grave. Sometimes, it's crazy what the effects of the death of a loved one can do, especially a son. I will wait until John needs my help for something, and I know what my answer will be. He didn't care how I felt; he never even asked if I was alright, so from now on when things arise that concern Daniel I will deal with them myself.

Friday 24th June 2005

I turned up as usual at the Albert Hotel. The atmosphere seemed more dynamic. Whilst singing my second song, a group of men came in. One of them, a dark skinned young man, winked at me. Politely I smiled back at him and carried on with my song. Afterwards, when sat at the bar, I was told that the dark skinned young man had bought me a drink. I was intrigued as to who he was. So, hoping to engage him in conversation, I walked to his table and thanked him. He invited me to sit down and we began to talk. As a child he used to live opposite one of my sisters. He asked me different things about my life; I don't think he believed I had written a book. We chatted for about an hour and when it was time for him to leave he said he'd like to meet me again, when he hoped we could pick up where we had left off. Although I seemed to get on very well with him I was still bemused by it all. I had no idea whether I would see him again, but I will certainly be looking out for him.

Saturday 2nd July 2005

It was 4 years ago today that Daniel was buried. I could not get myself together. When the clock reached 2 pm I blurted out,

"Well, we would be burying Daniel now."

That evening I went to the Spiritualist church but I didn't receive a message from the medium. However, one of the men I know told me that he had seen Daniel stood behind me. He told me what a proud young man he was, especially with his hair and he was so very "right". He also told me that my son finally knew that things people had said about me were all lies and he knows the truth. The man said that Daniel does love me and always has done. That information meant everything to me.

Tomorrow evening is my birthday party and I hope that everyone invited was looking forward to it. I will raise a glass to Daniel who will be there in spirit.

Sunday 3ʳᵈ July 2005

I'd been occupied for most of the morning preparing and cooking lunch as John was visiting me. The outfit I would wear at my birthday party was already laid out on the bed. Lunch passed without incident and John said that he would be at my party. Once the time reached 3 o'clock nerves and excitement combined to give me butterflies in my stomach. I had told my guests to arrive at the party from 8 pm onwards. The buffet would be at 9 pm.

John drove me to the Albert Hotel and when we arrived John's family and their friends and my friends from the Spiritualist church were already there. Within less than an hour the hotel was quite crowded. A couple that had lost their son about a year ago were there. It was great to be with everyone and to share my night with people who genuinely wished me well.

The time came for me to make some kind of announcement. I thought I had it all worked out but when I picked up the microphone everything vanished from my head. I managed to thank everyone and then announced that I would sing a special song, Daniel's song, "Somewhere Over the Rainbow". I thought it would be easy, especially as I had sung that song numerous times and recorded it too. How wrong could I be, how I got through it without breaking down, I will never know. My throat was dry, I felt weak and the power seemed to leave my voice. I think people understood, but the applause was muted.

Neil, who runs the karaoke, announced that the buffet was open. I had no idea what my cake would look like until the landlady walked into the room with all the candles lit. Everyone sang "Happy Birthday" and, in front of everyone, I had to blow out my candles. The last time I did that was on my 8th birthday. The cake was so beautiful and for the second time that evening I was speechless. I was overwhelmed and didn't want to cut it, I wanted to keep it whole and take it home. That cake was so precious to me.

The evening went without a hitch. There was never a hint of trouble, which says just what great friends I have. I may have had to wait 36 years for a party but it was worth it.

Thursday 7th July 2006,

The weather has been hot for quite a while now. As Thursday is my shopping day I give myself a treat going round as many stores as I can. Window-shopping can be great fun. Today I decided to look in the window of an ornament shop that occasionally I buy from. There was a sale on and in the window was what looked like a beautiful ornamental antelope. According to the card it had been reduced from £70 to £10. I asked the assistant if the price was correct, she said it was. It was so gorgeous that I just had to have it. The box it came in must have been worth £10.

John brought me home and together we opened the box. John's eyes lit up; even he liked what he saw. I still could not believe the price, what a bargain it was. My new ornament was given a prime spot on my marble mantle piece. I then had another look in the box and discovered a sealed envelope. Carefully I opened it, not knowing what to expect. My beautiful antelope was a collectable item. It was a limited edition and I had a certificate to prove it. How lucky could I be? Later in the day John called in and when I told him about my good fortune he didn't believe me. Then I showed him the documents.

The following day I decided to take another trip into town. John picked me up in the taxi and inquired what it was I needed to buy. I told him I felt lucky and was going to see if I could pick up any more bargains. The ornament shop sale was still on and in the window were 2 smaller animal figurines priced at £10 each. I went inside and the assistant remembered me from the day before. I asked her if there were any more ornaments of the same brand, which was "Red Earth".

She called the owner, explaining that I was the one who had purchased the antelope. The owner said that he did have a giraffe from the same collection but he thought it had been sold. Then he checked under the shelves and to his amazement and mine, it was still there. We agreed on £10 for it. Then he found smaller versions of a tiger, a lion and a zebra. I struck a deal with him by offering £21 for all 3, which he accepted.

My mantlepiece now looks like a splendid ornamental zoo. I adore anything like that and I know I had made a huge saving on the original prices. That evening, I went to the Albert Hotel and joined in a game of "play your cards right". I won £75. It crossed my mind to do the lottery.

Saturday 9ᵗʰ July 2005

One of my birthday presents was a computer. For several days I'd been trying to get connected to the Internet but couldn't do it. John had tried without success. Today, everything seemed to click.

I'd previously been warned that if I didn't understand what I was doing not to fiddle. I ignored the advice and just pressed a few buttons. As if by magic the Internet appeared. John was in the house and he had no idea what all the cheering was about until he came and looked. I could not understand why things were suddenly going right for me. Was it coincidence or something else?

I went to the Spiritualist church and there was a message from the medium. He asked if there had been a recent anniversary. I answered in the affirmative and he said that I had already had my fingers burnt or it was about to happen. Maybe it was the ornaments, had

I been taken for a ride? However, the ornaments had nothing to do with Daniel's anniversary so it couldn't have been them. The medium said whoever it was in "spirit" was sending me comfort, as he knew that deep down I was always hurting. I would just have to wait and see.

Over the next couple of weeks my life became becalmed. Nothing much happened until, on the evening of Monday 25th July, I decided to send a message to my friend who is in college. All I wanted to know was if he was alright. When he last came home he didn't contact me so I thought he might have some kind of problem. He had previously remarked that he was coming home to sort out his money problems. When I finally got in touch with him, he asked, "What had it got to do with me." I agreed and told him of my concern as a friend. His messages became nastier and eventually he asked if he could call me in 20 minutes, I agreed.

The conversation became increasingly abusive and then he hit where he knew it would really hurt by saying that at least his mother had never abandoned her children like I had abandoned mine. I was angry and hurt at what he had said. I explained that it was not entirely my fault that I had lost my family. He didn't seem to listen but kept telling me that everyone knew that I had abandoned my children. No matter how hard I tried to argue back, he had an answer for it. When the call had ended I burst into tears. I asked myself if it was my fault, did I hurt my children? John had told me that I would get hurt if I carried on contacting my friend but he had never been that cruel and nasty before. I wouldn't mind if what he had said was true, but none of it was. Well, I had had my fingers well and truly burnt.

Tuesday 26th July 2005

I'd bought a new ring with my winnings from "play your cards right" and today it was delivered. I ripped the top off the padded bag and, with great anticipation, opened the box. It was absolutely beautiful. I like the big chunky stones and this one was Lima Quartz and Aquamarine. It brightened up my day for a while.

Friday 29th July 2005

As was usual for a Friday I went to the Albert Hotel. I bought a drink and the girls behind the bar told me there was a spare stool at the end of the bar. I carried it to the centre of the bar where I like to sit. Then a man to the left of me said my name "Rosie, Rosie", a couple of times. I looked at him, but didn't recognise him so I ignored him. He asked why I wouldn't "take up" on a conversation with him. I asked him who he was but he insisted that I knew him, but I didn't. Then he told me things about myself, who I had been married to and that my ex husband had a new wife. He also said that he knew my brother and he'd read my book. He said that I had missed a lot out. Then he said things about my children. How could I possibly write about my love for them when it was not true? I could not understand why he was doing this; the encounter was turning into a major argument. He was making things up as he went along. His stories were complete fabrication so I stood my ground and argued back. He had an answer to everything. It was as if he had pre-planned it. When he went to the toilet I asked one of the local lads at the bar who he was and he told me. I'd never seen him in there before.

He returned and continued having a go at me. According to him I was known years ago as an easy lay and that he had even been in my home at the time. I knew that that was a complete lie. The altercation lasted for around an hour and a quarter then I turned my back on him and he left me alone. Not long afterwards he left. What he said to me was bad enough but what really upset me was that he'd insulted Daniel's memory, which was unforgivable.

The landlord and his wife had been out for the night and when they came back the landlord went behind the bar to help out. He asked me if I was alright, I said I wasn't and gave him an idea of what had happened. Before going home I explained everything to him. He said he would sort it out, so I left it at that.

Saturday 30th July 2005

John visited today. He wanted to know why I'd not phoned him the previous night to say that I was home safe. When I told him what had happened, the first thing he said was "you should have called me, I would have come round to the Albert Hotel." I am not a person who involves others if I can help it. John has too much to lose if he should get into trouble, with him being a taxi driver, he could even lose his license. I learnt a valuable lesson from that experience. If anyone tries to pull a stunt like that again I'll just walk away. However, it could be difficult when people you love are being dragged through the mud.

Sunday 31st July 2005

John and I had planned to go to the Albert Hotel tonight for a quiet drink. I phoned John and told him to make sure that he had something to eat beforehand. He is not a drinker and even the smallest amount can affect him. We met up in the bar and sat with one of my friends who told me that she was looking for somewhere to live. She was in the company of a man I thought I recognised. Evidently he was a family friend and she was staying with him until she could find somewhere of her own. John asked me if the man who had been offensive to me was in, I told him he wasn't. John was planning something but I wasn't sure what it was. After consuming three pints of beer it was apparent that he'd not eaten anything before coming out; I was so angry with him.

I still couldn't put a name or a place to the man who was sat with my friend. Yet I knew I had seen him somewhere. It had to be important for my mind to keep going back to it. I could see that John was getting drunk and warned him to space his drinks but he didn't want to listen. I knew what he was doing; he was hoping that the man who had been dragging up my past on Friday night would come in. John isn't a fighter so by getting drunk he'd made himself ready to challenge the man should he make an appearance. Even though I had told him not to get involved and that I could fight my own battles he would defend my reputation should the necessity arise.

When I could stand it no longer, I asked my friend's companion if I knew him. I told him that his face looked familiar and he said the same to me. As we talked I began to realise who he was.

"Are you a nurse?"

"Yes," he replied, "but not in this area." My pulse raced, I began to feel close to this man.

"Have you ever worked in this area, such as Bassetlaw Hospital."

"Yes, a few years ago." Now I knew who he was. All kinds of questions went through my mind. Why had I met with him now, or even at all? There had to be a reason.

"Do you remember me coming to you in the corridor of the hospital, and asking if you had my son there, and I told you his name was Daniel Footitt." I asked, almost stumbling over my words.

"Was that in A&E."

"Yes," I said, hardly able to contain my emotions.

"I remember," he said. He went on to say that he remembered asking if I was Daniel's mum and how he had showed me to a room where I could wait for news of my son's condition. He said he would never forget that night, as there had been two fatalities. There was nothing they could have done for Daniel, as his injuries were too severe. He told me his name was Brian and as we talked he asked if I would accept something. I had no idea what he meant, maybe some advice. Then he took the most beautiful crucifix from around his neck; it was attached to a string of gorgeous white mother of pearl beads. He passed it to me saying that he wanted me to have it. He told me that both a Bishop and a Priest had blessed it. I was overwhelmed, it was as if he had been sent by someone to tell me something.

I asked if he would give his telephone number to my friend, as I would like to stay in touch with him. By this time, John had drunk far too much and was becoming morose. Maybe I wasn't paying him enough attention. After all, he was only doing what he thought best and was ready to protect me should there be any trouble. The problem was he could hardly stand up.

Monday 1st August 2005

8.15 am, John always calls round to see me before starting work so I telephoned him to make certain that he was out of bed. I was worried about the amount of alcohol he'd consumed the previous evening. He sounded a bit groggy but said that he was OK. By 9.30 he hadn't arrived so I knew something was wrong. He was usually at my house well before then so I phoned him again. He said he couldn't move. I called his mum and told her that John was unwell and I'd go and look after him. He was really ill, the level of alcohol in his system was still very high.

Throughout the day I insisted that he drank lots of fluid and ate small amounts of easily digested food. By the end of the evening he'd recovered sufficiently enough for me to go home. Thank goodness he didn't drive at all today.

Wednesday 3rd August 2005

I called my Spiritualist friend Michael and told him about some of the things that had happened recently. I mentioned the male nurse who I had met in my local public house. I told him what we had talked about then showed him the necklace that he gave to me, saying that I would always treasure it. Michael told me that it was a Rosary. He commented how beautiful it was and what a great thing for that man to do. Michael also believed that there was a reason for the male nurse being there that night.

Today I had two wonderful pieces of jewellery delivered. One was a gorgeous blue topaz and garnet ring, the other an Indian garnet necklace. I can't wait to wear them this weekend.

Friday 5th August 2005

As the weekend approaches I am becoming more anxious about going to the Albert Hotel as the man who had slandered me may be there. Fortunately, he never came in but someone else did. It was a man who I had befriended some time previously but hadn't seen for a while. He made his way across to me. He'd been working away but gave no indication where. We chatted until it was my turn on the karaoke. Before going up to sing I asked him to wait because I wanted to continue our conversation, there was a lot to catch up on.

The songs went well and afterwards I looked around for my friend, but he had gone. It was great to see him but being an inquisitive person I would have liked to know more about where he'd been working, what he was doing now and whether he'd be in the Albert Hotel again. The whole thing was a bit of a mystery.

Sunday 7th August 2005

Today proved to be highly traumatic for me. I couldn't seem to focus on anything for very long. John came for lunch but I couldn't rid myself of the confusion that was building inside my head. For no reason I began to pick fights with John who took it all in his stride. After lunch he went home and then the real reason for my confused agitation became apparent. I had a major epileptic fit. Later, when I had recovered, I put on a new face and went to the Albert Hotel. I confided in the bar staff, telling them that should I collapse they had to get me out of there as quickly as possible.

Brian the Male Nurse and my friend were stood at the bar. They overheard the conversation and my friend asked where John was. I said he'd gone home. She knew about my epilepsy so she borrowed my mobile phone to call John, telling him of her concerns for me. Soon afterwards John arrived and I felt reassured just to have him there. He knows how insecure I get when I've had a seizure and I'm sure he understood why I'd been argumentative at lunchtime.

Instead of going out I should have been resting but life has to go on. I tried my best to sing, managing 3 songs but there was no power in my voice at all. Feeling unwell I went to the toilet where I took time to recover. On returning to the bar everyone was concerned. Brian took my pulse then gently scolded me for not resting. Being a nurse he knew that an epileptic fit takes a lot out of a person, particularly one who is slightly built.

When he was sure that I wasn't going to have another fit John went home, as he only lives around the corner, leaving me to finish my drink and relax with my friends. Later, he took me home in the taxi and said that he'd call and see me in the morning. True to his word he arrived. I must have looked awful, I felt as though I had been in a boxing ring. I told John that I was sorry about the things I'd said to him. He just shrugged his shoulders and said it was OK. I still can't get it out of my head why Brian has come into my life - it is such a mystery.

Tuesday 9th August 2005

Even though I already have one cat, Alfie who is female, I decided to have another one. Alfie is about 8 years old and I knew there would be some jealousy with her. I have a friend who fosters kittens and then rehomes them and she brought two round for me to see. We were interested in seeing how my cat would react to having a kitten around the place. The kitten I chose was a longhaired tabby and by coincidence Alfie has a "boyfriend" who is a tabby that visits her every day.

Of course there was lots of growling and hissing noises from my cat, this was her house and she was the boss. This didn't in the slightest bit bother the kitten as he explored his way around the living room. I suppose my cat felt threatened but I knew that I had to make just as much fuss of her as I would the new one. I decided to let Alfie outside after a few hours, but by the afternoon she had returned home and ate the kitten's food.

Wednesday 10th August 2005

Things couldn't be going better. Alfie seems to have more or less taken to the kitten. There is still some jealousy there but I'm certain that in time it will go. I have named the kitten Tigger, as I think it suits his personality.

Thursday 11ᵗʰ August 2005

Today, whilst walking round Retford town centre, I met one of Daniel's friends. He told me he was a dad now and showed me a photograph of his baby. I was happy for him yet my thoughts turned to Daniel and I remarked that maybe he would have been a dad too. There was no bitterness in me, just a sadness that never goes away.

I'd left the kitten in the kitchen and when I arrived back he was curled up fast asleep. I don't think he'd even missed me yet all I had done was worry whether he was alright or not. As each day passes Alfie is getting used to the idea of another cat in the house. Tigger is learning when to back off but she will eat whatever Alfie leaves in his food bowl.

Sunday 14ᵗʰ August 2005

In my bedroom I have a large photograph of my dad, so whilst getting ready to go to the Albert Hotel I decided to take a photo of it with my camera phone. I'd already taken a similar picture of Daniel and now I had images of both the men I loved, to carry everywhere with me.

During my karaoke spot the D.J. took several photos of me at different times with his digital camera. He showed me something I had never seen before; there were "spirit orbs" above my head. This amazed me, particularly as one of them was really big in size. There is a story going round that other people have experienced similar things in the Albert Hotel, yet my feeling was that they were the two men that I loved so much in my life, my son and my dad. The D.J. told me that they were like Spirit Guides.

Later, when I arrived home, I looked for the kitten; he was nowhere to be seen. I had shut them in the kitchen together, so he had to be somewhere. Alfie was waiting for me, but Tigger had vanished. I became quite worried, as I knew that he couldn't get outside. After a good search, I happened to move the curtain behind my computer, and there he was, looking so innocent, but just how he had jumped that high I shall never know. I was so relieved to see him that I just cuddled him. At least he hadn't come to any harm.

Friday 19th August 2005

I was getting ready to go to the Albert Hotel when a knock came at my door. I wasn't expecting anyone so I was surprised to see a young girl who I knew. Her parents own a café and she didn't look too happy. I invited her in and asked what was wrong. Her father is not English and has different ways and principles to English folk. I can understand that but I can also understand his daughter's frustrations too. I told her to come to the Albert Hotel with me; I knew that she would be safe and wouldn't be wandering around town on her own.

We had a good chat and she seemed to enjoy having time to herself. After a while she told me that she was going to try and sort things out with her dad, but he had to make the effort to apologise. I said that if her dad admitted that he was wrong, she should accept that. Her dad is a proud man and at least it would be a start if they began talking. Then, as I turned my head away from her my heart sank. There in front of the bar was the man who had previously insulted me. The landlord noticed my annoyance and asked what was wrong. I told him that the man was there and should he start anything he would get my drink over him. He reassured me that the man would behave himself and he didn't want any trouble.

The evening went smoothly and no comments were passed. The young girl finally left and I told her that at if at any time she should need me just to call.

Sunday 21st August 2005

This evening the D.J. who had taken the photographs brought them in to the Albert Hotel. I was amazed when I saw them and felt that the orbs above my head were more than just a trick of the light - they had a meaning for me. Not long afterwards the young girl who had been with me on the Friday night reappeared. She said she couldn't leave without saying thank you and goodbye. She explained that she had new accommodation and a job but had to move away from home. Before she left I sang a duet with Neil the D.J. We performed "Endless Love", a song that I had recorded on one of my albums.

It was now time for the young girl to leave. It was hard to say goodbye, as I have known her for some time, even Neil was impressed with her.

Earlier in the day John visited and had his usual Sunday lunch. Afterwards an argument broke out between us. He said that getting a new kitten would destroy the older cat. I wasn't sure what he meant by this, it was nonsense but it didn't stop me feeling guilty.

The following morning the person who sold me the kitten telephoned to say she would collect him for his injections the next day. I was unsure whether to mention what John had said or not. I chose not to. Soon afterwards the phone rang again, she had forgotten to tell me what time she would be coming. There was something about my tone of voice that told her things weren't right. It was then I told here what had happened; I couldn't stop myself from crying. She said that the choice was mine whether to give him up or not. I knew if I kept the kitten and Alfie suffered as a consequence, John would never let me hear the last of it, so I decided to give him up. The woman said she would come and collect Tigger at 5.30 pm, but once he'd gone, there would be no turning back.

I'd been crying for most of the day when they came to collect him. The woman did say that I could give Tigger a cuddle and say goodbye to him. I had become so attached to this tiny animal in such a short time. He was put straight into the box and taken out. I never had the chance to say goodbye let alone cuddle him. After they'd gone it was like another loss to me, I sobbed like I did when Daniel died.

Wednesday 24th August 2005

Sitting at my computer I thought of all the wrong and hurtful things I had done, not intentionally but still bad enough to offend and hurt someone. At the forefront of my mind was the young man I used to sing with. The things I had said to him led to a serious confrontation and it was now a month since we had spoken. I didn't want it to end there so initially I thought about emailing him but decided that would be too impersonal, so I decided to telephone instead. We spoke briefly but he was still annoyed and hurt at what I had said to him previously so we left it there.

I went out for a while and a few minutes following my return the phone rang, it was the BT messaging service telling me I had missed a call. It was my former singing partner who said he knew I would call eventually. I couldn't apologise to him enough for the things I had said. Good friends are hard to come by and I think he knew I valued his friendship. I said I wanted to stay in touch. To my surprise and relief he agreed.

Friday 26th August 2005

After a morning in town I sat in the taxi office waiting for John to take me home. Whilst waiting, the door opened and a woman came in. She spoke to John's mother and had the accent of a true Romany gypsy, just like the ones that my dad travelled with in his younger days.

"You're a Romany gypsy," I said. She agreed but added that she was not like those who tell fortunes at fairgrounds but she did tell me what a bad past I'd had and I should try and put it all behind me and move on. She told me I had not had it easy and to stop being soft with people, as they were walking all over me. She also said that I could be whatever I wanted to be. I asked her if she had anything that I could buy. I chose a small trinket. When she had left I looked at my purchase, it was a small water globe with glitter and a star inside with the words "wishes do come true" on its side. I felt different once I had spoken to her, a lot stronger and more determined than ever.

That evening, whilst I was in my local public house, something extraordinary happened. There were a lot of new faces in the bar, mainly men. One of them came to the corner where I was sat and began talking to a girl at the next table. He kept looking across as if he knew me. His face seemed familiar but where from I wasn't sure. He said that he recognised me from the newspapers, it would have been when my book was published or when I recorded my albums. He asked my name and when I told him he said that he used to work with my brother who he thought a lot of. I didn't get into a conversation with him regarding my book or it's contents. He was a charming man but the wedding ring on his finger cautioned me to keep my distance; I had to make it clear that I was not interested in married men. I told him to treasure what he had at home. The conversation carried on quite normally once I had put him straight on a few things.

In the same group there was another man who began to chat to me. He was older than the first one and when he found out who I was he said that he thought he knew my dad. I showed him the photo I have on my phone and he asked where it was taken. I said that it was behind a pub that used to be in Retford but had since been knocked down. That jolted his memory and he said that he remembered him.

My last two songs of the night were "The Wonder Of You" and "I Believe". The crowd sung along with me, it was such a boost for my confidence. My taxi arrived and I kissed both men in a friendly way. I said it was nice to have met them and went home. I felt quite proud of myself; I'd made new friends and also felt like a proper singer for a while.

Saturday 27th August 2005

I felt a strong inclination to call my two daughters in Scotland. Call it instinct but that evening I dialled the number nervously, thinking that something was wrong. This feeling was compounded when a voice mail service on the end of the main house phone invited me to leave a message. I was angered by this as the conditions of the adoption was that I was informed regularly of their progress and that I received up to date photographs. Keeping my anger in check I left a message for the family to get in touch or to send some photos. All I could think of was that they had fallen out with me for some reason.

The next day I was thinking more rationally and called the adoptive mother of my daughters. I asked if she had received my message. She explained that I hadn't given her my phone number when I had it changed and asked me what was wrong; I burst into tears saying that I thought she had fallen out with me. We agreed for her to send me a few pictures by email and eventually I received a photograph of my eldest daughter. I couldn't believe how much she had grown.

Wednesday 31st August 2005

I had promised the young girl from the café that I would help to make her new house look clean and lived in. It was the hottest day so far this year and I chose to clean and scrub the kitchen whilst she did the bathroom. Between us we would sort out her bedroom. Even with all the windows open it was stifling; the work seemed to go on forever. I used all kinds of cleaning solutions and eventually, after 4 hours, the house was clean and fresh.

I live in the same street as this young girl and walked home just after 6 pm. An hour later she came to my house with a "take away" meal for our tea. I was ravenous; cleaning her house was hard work. When she had gone I fell asleep, I was exhausted, I didn't realise how unfit I was. Usually it takes me forever to go to sleep, I will wake 3-4 times through the night. This night I slept through till morning. It's amazing what a bit of exercise can do.

Thursday 1st September 2005

My friend in Scotland called to say that she had sent another e-mail containing photos of my daughters. My girls were now young women and not babies anymore. In the evening John visited and I showed the pictures to him and, like me, he couldn't believe how they had changed. The last time he had seen the girls was when they were very small. I sent my friend an e-mail to let her know the photos had come through and what I thought.

Friday 2nd September 2005

Today I called my friend in Scotland and bombarded her with questions about my daughters. Although I still miss them I don't really know them at all now. So, as long I have regular photos and information about their well being I will be happy, for the time being anyway.

In the evening the Albert Hotel was full of customers; they couldn't all be there to hear me sing. Evidently it was a cricket presentation - after the trophies had been presented and speeches made the crowd thinned out a little. I was given free reign at the karaoke and it turned out to be a good night.

Later on at home I sat for a while before going to bed. My mind wandered back over the evening. It was good that I could sing in public but my horizons were limited to the Albert Hotel and the karaoke. I was also becoming dissatisfied with other parts of my life, so decisions had to be made. The first thing I had to do was finish the relationship with John. He was just using me. It was convenient for him to come round for his creature comforts but that had to stop, otherwise my life would be on permanent hold.

Saturday 3rd September 2005

John is coming to me for his Saturday lunch; he will be here all day tomorrow as well. I know if I don't do something about it no one else will. It will be difficult because when I tell him that I want him out of my life he won't accept it. He will give me the benefit of his own views on what I should do in such a dictatorial way that a row will blow up. The whole thing has gone well beyond a joke. I am certain that he thinks there is still a relationship between us. Although I am determined not to go down that road again I decided to put off the confrontation until another time.

Tuesday 6th September 2005

For the past two days I have felt unwell and seem to be sleeping more than usual. I am falling asleep during the day and then sleeping through the night, waking up in the morning with a severe headache. I did wonder if I was building up to another seizure but the feelings are different. I slept for approximately 7 hours last night and when John visited I don't think he believed me when I explained just how ill I felt. It was as if my head was about to explode. John went home at about 11 pm and told me he would see me the following day. I had to go straight to bed or I would just fall asleep downstairs.

Wednesday 7th September 2005

At 1.30 am the phone at the side roused me. I was groggy but managed to answer it. The caller was John asking how I was, he sounded worried. He said he knew what I meant by having such a bad headache as he was now suffering in the same way. He said he thought he knew what was causing it and would come round straight away; he didn't want to take any chances. He'd remembered that I'd previously mentioned that the gas fire smelt really odd and I thought it was giving off fumes. He'd also remembered that I'd mentioned that the fire made a peculiar noise when I tried to light it. I went downstairs to let him in and he stayed with me for the rest of the night. In the morning he called the service engineer. Although he was booked to come and service the fire at the beginning of the following month it obviously couldn't be left until then.

Taking the phone from John I explained to the engineer what had been happening, even Alfie my cat was sleeping all the time. The engineer said that the earliest he would be able to come was Friday 9th, so he recommended that I call British Gas and report it as an emergency. I did this and was told not to strike a match or use a cigarette lighter in the house, to open all the windows and turn off the gas at the meter. It's only when faced with a gas leak that you realise how dangerous it can be. An engineer from British Gas was soon on the scene and I explained the problem to him. I mentioned the noise made by the fire when it was turned on and he looked concerned. He turned the gas on at the meter and lit the fire. He said something was definitely wrong and told me not to use it until it had been thoroughly serviced. A warning sticker was fixed to the front of the fire. Perhaps now I'll get rid of my headache and Alfie will return to her regular sleep pattern.

I decided to go into town and phoned for a taxi. I didn't feel much like walking around so I went to the post office and the bakery then made my way back to the taxi office. Whilst having a drink with John's mum, a young woman came in; I must say I barely recognised her. It was Donna, one of my best friends from North Wheatley Primary School. She told John's mum how her mum used to knit for us as children. Seeing her brought back many memories. She knew about Daniel and that I had recorded a song for him. I said that I would send her a copy of my album.

I also mentioned that I had written a book and that a lot of it was about my brother abusing me. A look of sadness came over her face as she told me that people had often speculated about things that may or may not have been going on between my brother and me but no one did anything about it. She wanted to stay in touch and gave me her address and phone number. I promised to get her a copy of my book.

Thursday 8th September 2005

This seemed to be a week for surprise meetings because today I called in to see Clare at her shop. Clare had kindly agreed to put my book on display and I picked up a copy to give to Donna. It was in Clare's shop that I met someone who had been my next-door neighbour ten years ago. We went into the café next to Clair's shop to catch up on what had been happening in our lives. During our conversation a woman entered the café, She came across to our table and said hello to my former neighbour. I thought nothing of it until we got up to leave.

Whilst I was paying the bill the two women became engrossed in conversation and I was sure they were discussing me. The woman who had made herself known to my former neighbour asked if I remembered her. She had a familiar face but I couldn't place her. I explained that there were many things from my past that I had blocked out and she said she could understand why. It transpired that she once lived on the same street as my family and from what she told me there were more people than I realised who had suspicions of what was happening behind the closed doors of the Shannon household. It just confirmed to me that where the abuse of children is concerned there are many people who are quite happy to bury their heads in the sand.

Whilst in town I called in at the shop from where I buy my cigarettes. To free up my hands to pay for them I placed my book on the counter. The young woman who usually serves me noticed the title and asked me about it. She was surprised to learn that I was the author and asked if she could have a look at it. She read the blurb on the back of the cover, burst into tears and ran out of the shop into a room at the back. Obviously something was seriously wrong so I followed her. She was so upset but wouldn't tell me why; I didn't want to pry so I could only speculate what had caused her so much distress.

That evening, I telephoned Donna and told her that I had a copy of my book for her. I offered to take it to her personally and she agreed. Donna and myself were very close as children and amazingly we were able to pick up from where we had left off all those years ago. I took both of my albums, as she had not heard them. Donna introduced her partner and children then we began talking and didn't stop until John called to collect me at 10 pm. We agreed to stay in touch.

I'd just about got my coat off when Donna rang. She couldn't stop reading my book and was on page 5 already. John left and I went to bed at around 11.45 pm. At 1 am my phone rang, it was Donna again; she had to let me know that she had finished reading my book and was amazed by its contents. We spoke for a while then she said that she would be in touch again.

Monday 12ᵗʰ September 2005

John called to take me into town, he was so stressed that I immediately began to worry. I asked what was wrong. He told me that I must not go into the taxi office, as I would not be welcome. This came as a bit of a shock and I asked him why. He said it was the way I kept my appearance. John also said my lifestyle may be causing some resentment or envy amongst others in the office. This made no sense to me, how could the way I live be of any concern to anyone. Certainly, taxi drivers can refuse to carry certain people, usually habitual drunks or those with a history of violence but I'd never heard of anyone being banned because of their appearance or moderate lifestyle. I made it clear to him that using a taxi was my choice not his and unless I heard to the contrary that is how it would stay.

This piece of nonsense was the opening I had been waiting for and that evening I decided to make the break from John. I reminded him of our earlier conversation and told him that perhaps my lifestyle should change, as I couldn't go on living the way I was. There was no relationship between us so what reason had he for visiting all of the time. I'd known for a while that he was using me to fill in his spare time. Keeping my emotions in check I remained calm throughout. He didn't like it but I had to be honest with him as it was beginning to ruin my life.

Wednesday 14ᵗʰ September 2005

I called into the music shop where my albums were on sale. This was just to see how sales were going and to pick up one or two for people who had asked me for them. There was a young woman in the shop who asked if I remembered her. I didn't immediately recognise her until she reminded me that I was in Clair's shop the day she called in to buy my book. By coincidence we had both lost someone close, she her partner and me, Daniel so I asked the shop owner to play a few tracks from my album. She purchased one and I told her that I would make sure received a copy of my first album. We exchanged phone numbers then went our separate ways.

Later on in the evening I telephoned my singing partner who features on my albums. He was telling me how busy he had been at college, and when I told him that John was now out of my life, he was amazed. He said he was surprised it had taken so long. Then he said that whilst out shopping he'd heard a song being played that we had recorded and we reminisced about the good times we'd had making the albums.

Friday 16ᵗʰ September 2005

This evening the Albert Hotel was busy so I stood at the bar with Neil and another man who I had seen there several times. There was a great atmosphere building up and with each song I sang I felt so much stronger inside. Eventually we managed to get seats at the bar and as we talked I began to laugh as I had never laughed before. I felt liberated; my face was aching. All kinds of emotions were going through my body, yet I didn't know why.

Near the end of the night one of the men who I was sat with, who I knew really well, began a conversation. His name was Tom and he thought I was still attached to John but once I had made it clear that there was nothing between us, things became even more relaxed. I enquired whether he was married and felt bad when he told me that he'd been a widower for five years. He volunteered that he had a daughter.

We carried on talking and at the end of the night the Frank Sinatra classic "My Way" was being performed and we both began singing it. Whilst still sat on our stools I found myself swaying in Tom's arms. His friend said that we weren't doing it properly, to get up and dance, so we did. I felt so happy and free. My taxi came and I said that I would have to go but would be there on Sunday as usual. I kissed him politely and a few more people got a kiss as well. I hoped that he didn't think that he'd frightened me off in any way. He was a really nice respectable guy and all the way home I felt butterflies fluttering inside me. Once I was home, I felt so different inside, as if I had come "alive". I had no idea where it would lead, only time would tell.

Saturday 17th September 2005

Today I went to the Spiritualist church and the medium was really great. She gave a message to a lady who was sat behind me, saying that someone in spirit had a birthday in the near future and she could hear the song "Danny Boy" being sung. I looked across at Michael, mouthing my son's name and he nodded. I left it until she had ended her service before going to speak to the medium. I explained it would have been my son Daniel's birthday on October 2nd and that the song "Danny Boy" was played at his funeral. She held my hands and asked how he had died. I said it was in a car crash. She explained that the message must have been for me, she could feel it and began to weep. In a strange way the medium's sadness comforted me.

This evening I told Michael about my feelings regarding the man I had danced with in the Albert Hotel and he told me to take things a step at a time. This was good advice; I didn't want to get hurt again, it had happened too many times before.

Sunday 18th September 2005

I walked into the Albert Hotel with a spring in my step. Tom was sat at the bar and I went over and sat beside him. We talked and laughed, I felt marvellous. As usual I sang a few songs and at the end of the night Neil performed a song called "Don't Close your

Eyes". While he was singing another man asked me to dance. I politely refused because the only person I wanted to dance with was still sat at the bar. A little further into the song, when a few others were dancing, I asked Tom if he would dance with me. Neil sang "Wonderful Tonight", and "Endless Love" and we danced to these, it was bliss. When the girl behind the bar told me that my taxi was outside I felt disappointed, I wanted my happiness to go on all night.

I felt so close to him whilst we were dancing and before leaving the hotel I kissed him, not just a peck on the cheek but a real full-blooded kiss. It felt great. I gave him my phone number and told him to call me and that I would be at the Albert Hotel again next week. I couldn't sleep for thinking about all we had talked about and the laughs we'd had. He seemed to be a down to earth type of guy, intelligent and interesting. The next day I asked Clair if I looked happy. She said I did, but wanted to know what had happened to make me so lighthearted. I told her about this new man and she said that I should go for it and get John out of my life once and for all.

Tuesday 20th September 2005

I have not heard from Tom yet. I do hope that I hadn't either frightened him off or rushed him into anything too soon.

I told John not to visit me anymore. If I wanted a relationship with another man it wouldn't look good if John turned up whenever he chose to. When I told him not to bother coming to see me again, he said

"Not even tonight?"

"No." I replied.

I also made it clear in a text message that his morning visits were out of the question as well. My life is my own and John will no longer dictate how I will live it.

Thursday 22nd September 2005

My mobile phone rang a couple of times and I thought this was the call I had been waiting for but it wasn't, someone had probably misdialed a number because the caller rang off without speaking. All day long I was like a cat on hot bricks. Maybe I was afraid of what would lay ahead the following night when I went to the hotel.

Friday 23rd September 2005

This morning I called in to see Clair and she thought the phone call could have been from Tom; only he wouldn't know what to say. I felt so full of myself and confident, I knew that tonight would tell the story.

Whilst waiting for my taxi I have to admit that I felt apprehensive, in fact I was a little scared. When I walked into the bar there he stood, in his usual place, but I still had to face him. I said "hello", as I normally would and everything seemed to fall into place after that. A group of men at the bar asked me if I wanted a stool. I thanked them and asked if another one was free. They laughed, one of them made a comment about me being greedy. We both sat down and together we had such a great time.

The evening passed very quickly and we ended up kissing and cuddling at the bar. People were watching, some out of curiosity and others who were talking about us. It didn't worry me, I was on my own cloud nine and that was all that mattered. In fun, the landlord asked if we wanted a room for the night. All I could do was laugh, though Tom went a little shy. I asked the landlord if we were offending him. He said "no" so we carried on, oblivious to anyone or anything outside our little corner of happiness.

Fifteen minutes before my taxi would be arriving I asked him to come outside with me. As we left the hotel, comments were made inferring that we were going home together. I pointed to his pint on the bar, making it clear that he was returning once I had gone. I still cannot believe how this man has made me feel, I am alive and vibrant. I asked him if he would call me when he got home. Even though he said he would, how could I be sure? I lay in bed unable to sleep and just after 2 am my phone rang. It was him. We talked for what seemed an age and that night I slept more soundly than I had done for a long time, so all I can say is he must be doing something right.

Saturday 24th September 2005

Like a pair of teenagers we exchanged messages on our phones all day. It was exhilarating. That evening, when I arrived at the Albert Hotel, the bar was full and he wasn't stood at his usual place. I thought maybe he hadn't come yet but there he was, sat at a table. I sat with him, talking and singing along to the disco. A few people moved away from the bar, making room for us to sit there. Friends said how pleased they were for us, which made us feel good too.

Ten minutes before my taxi was due to arrive we went outside. We leant up against the wall kissing, I knew something was different; his kiss was more passionate, more confident. I couldn't believe how this made me feel. Earlier in the bar he told me that he wanted to get "behind my eyes". I wasn't really certain what he meant by this but I assumed he wanted to know me better. Reluctantly, I got into my taxi and went home.

Later, he called me and I asked him about it. He said that when he looks into my eyes something seems to draw him closer to me. Maybe that's my body's way of telling him that I want him. I asked if he had mentioned me to his daughter and he said that he had. I will be seeing him again tomorrow night and then comes the big test. On Monday afternoon he and his daughter are coming to my house. He wants to show me off to her. I am a bit scared but it should all be alright. I must just remember to take things slowly; these things can't be rushed. We arranged that once this meeting was over and his daughter had returned home he would come back to my house that evening. We can have some privacy and get to know each other better. I don't know what the outcome of this will be, but all I can hope for is that things work out.

Sunday 25 September 2005

Despite my insistence that John should stay out of my life he called round to see me today. I told him that I was seeing someone else, but he already knew. Retford is a small town so the word had circulated and being a taxi driver he picks up all the gossip; he'd even heard tittle tattle about who Tom was, but I said nothing.

In the afternoon I received a message from Tom to say he was ill, he must have picked up a virus or something. I phoned him and he sounded quite poorly but said he would still meet me at the hotel. I didn't think it was a good idea for him to be out but it was his choice. I arrived much earlier than him and when he came in and walked over to me he looked dreadful. His temperature was obviously raised and he was sweating profusely. I felt helpless, as I couldn't do anything for him. It takes him nearly an hour to walk home and I wasn't about to let him do that. He shared my taxi and I made sure he was dropped off at his house before I went home. At least I knew he would be in the warm and could go straight to bed.

He called me before he went to sleep saying how ill he felt. I just wished I could have been with him. I thought about him for some time before falling to sleep. The next morning I awoke with a sore throat.

Monday 26th September 2005

It is 11.30 am and Tom hasn't called me yet, I just hope he's alright. I won't phone him in case he is still in bed. It was just after lunch when he phoned to say he was no better.

By mid afternoon I was feeling really ill, coughing, and my throat felt like it had been cut with glass. My eyes were watering and I called the doctor's surgery to make an appointment. I was in luck, there had been a cancellation and I could see my own G.P later that evening. Whatever the infection was it had gone straight to my chest and I was prescribed a course of strong antibiotics. I couldn't stop coughing; even the pharmacist commented that I looked in a bad way. I felt it too. I asked for some ointment for my eyes, as they were really sore. I was given a preparation containing liquid paraffin, which seemed to work.

Upon returning home I sent a text to Tom, letting him know what the doctor had said. Later I called him and despite my sore throat I couldn't stop talking. He is so different in every way to anyone else I have been out with. I was on the phone for about an hour and a half, but who cares. I think about him all night, which is how I know my feelings for him are more than just surface. But scared that one or both of us might get hurt, I'll take each day one at a time.

Tuesday 27th September 2005

I was impatient, waiting for him to get in touch. When it got to 1 pm I began to worry; he could have taken a turn for the worse so I called him. I have to admit that I miss him; I love to hear his voice. He said that he was feeling a bit better and was going into town as he had some things to collect. He would contact me when he returned home. We spoke about him and his daughter rearranging the visit and he told me that he would discuss it with her.

The visit was rescheduled for this Thursday afternoon. I can't begin to explain how I feel about him. We have so much in common too. Earlier, I had told him about Daniel, who's birthday it would have been this week and he asked which school my son went to. When I said Tuxford Comprehensive and that I went there also, he told me that he did too, which I found to be such a coincidence.

Up to this stage I had not told him about my book or happenings in my past life that he should know about if our relationship was to grow. That evening, when he phoned, I told him that he should read my book but first I wanted to talk to him about things in my life that should come from me and not from someone else. He already knew about Daniel and about my brother abusing me.

I chose to tell him about my other children this evening, and how my daughters came to be living with their Godmother. Also that I had run away to

Scotland where I had another child. After telling him this I thought it was time to change the subject, he could probably take only so much, particularly as there was more to come. My life story didn't seem to bother him and he confirmed that he and his daughter would visit as planned.

Wednesday 28th September 2005

I arrived home from shopping and sent a text to Tom asking if the visit was still going ahead. He replied, saying that they would arrive at 2 pm. I was absolutely dreading it, but then again how must his daughter have been feeling. I was the adult here; so I must act like one. The knock came at my door, I answered it and invited them inside. Tom's daughter was beautiful, so poised and mature looking for an 18 year old. I showed them through to the living room and they both commented how comfortable it looked. I made some tea and we sat chatting for a while. Then I took them on a grand tour of the house and they seemed to like it. Even Alfie greeted them in her own way. The nerves had long since gone and we all seemed to get along very well. It was 5.30 pm when they left and I told his daughter that I hoped to meet her again.

It was 7.15 pm when I received a text from Tom asking if I was happy with the way things went. I replied, saying that I was relieved it went so well and that he had a daughter to be proud of. He replied, saying that his daughter thinks I'm great, and pretty as well. I not sure about me being pretty but all compliments are welcome. This was a big step and we'll see how things go from here.

Friday 30th September 2005

The florists delivered Daniel's birthday flowers. They were so nice and my eyes misted over with tears. I told the young delivery girl how pleased I was with them. She asked how I was keeping, I said I was OK and asked her to come inside until I paid her for them. I became increasingly upset and she gave me a hug before leaving. I asked her to thank everyone that had worked on the flowers as they always make them special for me.

Once she had left I had a really good cry, then booked a taxi to take me to the cemetery. There was no way I could go on his birthday, as it would be far too painful. That evening I knew I had to keep myself occupied and went to the Albert Hotel. Tom came in and seeing him made me feel better.

My ex partner John has a half sister who I like. I'd told her of Tom and asked her to join us at the hotel that night. Tom said he didn't mind and looked forward to meeting her. She came in and gave me a hug and the evening went really well. When she left we had the remainder of the night together, it was wonderful just to hold him and be close to him. He makes me feel alive and wanted.

When my taxi arrived I said that we could take him home first, as I wasn't about to take any chances with his health. Yesterday I had given him my book and a tape of the live interview I did on Radio Nottingham. I was pleased that I had told him things about my past, so it wouldn't come as a shock when he read the book.

Saturday 1st October 2005

We arrived at the Albert Hotel almost together. Tom told me that he was on chapter 5 of my book. He'd reached the bit where my mother first began to turn from a loving mother to a bitter and twisted person. The disco was on and the young man that runs it was so comical. Our stomachs were hurting as we laughed. Peanuts were flying in different directions and hitting people. We knew that it was the D.J. who was doing it; it was hilarious.

Midway through the night we began to kiss and I felt wonderful. It's not just the way that he holds me but everything about him I love. He looked into my eyes and said, "You do know I'm crackers about you, don't you."

I told him that the feeling was mutual. We held each other until my taxi arrived. As we parted company I asked him to phone me later, I just wanted to hear his voice again before going to sleep. It wasn't long before my phone was ringing. Eventually, we had to say goodnight to each other yet again. I just wish he had been there to hold me. As I lay in bed I thought only of him. Then I fell asleep.

Sunday 2nd October 2005

Today would have been Daniel's birthday. As always my mind drifted to when he was a little boy playing on his toy tractor, so innocent. Tears are never far away, how I wished he were here.

I sent Tom a text message telling him what time I'd got up. He replied some time after 10 am, saying that he'd just got out of bed. I returned one to him saying I would call him later in the day and calling him a lazy blighter. We are just like a pair of teenagers and it's wonderful. Things just seemed to get better and we were becoming more open about things. He was so easy to talk to. Normally, I wouldn't be so forthcoming about my life or my feelings but I knew that I loved this gentle fellow more than any other man in my life, apart from Daniel and my dad.

This evening, in the Albert Hotel, I could feel my feelings for him strengthening. We sat at the bar and talked, then I chose a few songs to sing from the karaoke book. One of them was called "Amazed" and whilst I was singing it I wanted him to listen to the words. Afterwards, he told me that he was sure the song was for us. We couldn't stop kissing but at one point he asked if I was going off him.

"Of course not," I told him gently. I don't know why he felt like that, but I was a little quieter than usual. Probably I was feeling guilty for being so happy and enjoying myself on Daniel's birthday.

When singing from the karaoke I normally watch the words on the screen or look at the ceiling. Not tonight, I found myself singing the songs to Tom. It was something I'd have never done before. Soon afterwards, Neil the DJ sang the song that we had both danced to when our relationship had first begun. He said that this was now our song. It is a beautiful ballad called "Don't Close Your Eyes Let It Be Me". Well, we hugged and kissed each other and didn't care if people were watching.

When it was time to go Neil came across to us and offered to do the disco at our wedding. Then the landlord said the reception had to be held in the Albert Hotel. The bar staff offered to be my bridesmaids. I was on such a high that I felt drunk, yet all I that had passed my lips was fruit juice. In the taxi we kissed and made the most of what little time we had before reaching his house. I asked him to call me later. We said things to each other that were so special. I told him that I would never hurt him. He repeated over and over again that he wanted to look after me and then he almost stammered the words "I love you." Without hesitation I told him that I loved him too. Everything was just perfect. He is coming to my house tomorrow evening and we can have some privacy to talk, listen to music and just be together. I can't wait to hold him in my arms.

Monday 3rd October 2005

At exactly 7.20 pm Tom arrived. I'd been watching the clock all day; it seemed to move slower and slower.

We went through to the living room where we held each other so tightly I thought my ribs would break. The evening was wonderful; we talked, drank tea and cuddled. It was as if I had known him all my life, I didn't want it to end, yet the time passed quickly and he soon had to return home to his daughter. It's strange how clocks seem to speed up when you don't want them to. I know he will never hurt me, abuse or bully me and most of all play mind games with me as others have done. He is the most caring and kindest man that I have ever had a relationship with and there's no way that I am going to let him go now I have found him. It will be his birthday soon and he's going to get a present that will show him just how much I love him.

Wednesday 5th October 2005

I collected Tom's present from the jewellers, hoping that he'd like it. Later, he and his daughter were calling to see me and I wanted to be ready for them. The shopping was put away in record time and I went round with the duster. On arrival I sat him in the living room and took his daughter into the kitchen where I showed her the gift I'd bought for her father. Just by her reaction I knew that I'd chosen wisely. She said he would be delighted with the Zippo lighter embossed with the words "Harley Davidson" that I'd bought. For him, it would be the perfect gift. I put it in my handbag where it will stay until his birthday. As always the clock determines all things. It doesn't seem fair to have to keep saying goodbye.

Thursday 6th October 2005

The hours seemed to drag by until I met Tom again. When I arrived at the Albert Hotel things were just great between us, I had his birthday present in my handbag. His card was left in the glove compartment of the taxi for when we went home. Halfway through the evening I noticed a change in him, it puzzled me. Why wouldn't he look at me, or didn't he want to? I began to question myself, had I done something to make him behave in this strange way? I asked him what was wrong, but he told me that he would rather keep it to himself for a while. I couldn't work it out what had upset him, but something had. Eventually, because I wouldn't let it drop and wanted to know, he told me. It was his insecurity again. He was worried because he thought another man fancied me. I had my suspicions of who this man might be but Tom was my number one and I told him so. He began to cheer up and the evening became relaxed and enjoyable.

At two minutes past midnight I wished him "happy birthday". I watched as he opened his present, he really liked it. I knew from the look on his face that I'd made the right choice. Later, as he prepared to get out of the taxi, the driver passed him his birthday card and I asked him to call me as usual then kissed him goodnight. He said he was upset about doubting me earlier in the evening and was happy that the other man meant nothing to me. This is what love is all about, a couple must learn to talk things through and share their emotions, good or bad. Patience is one of my strong points and I am determined to make this relationship work. I even told him on the phone that if he got down on his knees in front of a bar full of people and asked me to be with him forever, I would say "yes".

Last week I e-mailed my daughters' adoptive mother in Scotland, enquiring how everyone was. I mentioned Tom and said how happy I was. The reply was not what I had expected. She said not to take it the wrong way but she found it difficult to understand why a man would want a woman who was always ill. I think she meant my epilepsy, but I wasn't sure so I phoned her to ask for some clarification. She knew that much of my past life had been blocked out of my mind but when she inferred that I had once been diagnosed as having Munchausen's Disease I was shocked, particularly as I had never heard of it. Then she told me the symptoms.

Someone with this disorder repeatedly pretends to have a severe illness so as to obtain medical treatment. In severe cases this attention seeking behaviour can involve another person, usually a child who may or may not be harmed in the process. This is Munchausen's Disease by Proxy. I was devastated and confused. Never before had anyone accused me of this. My epilepsy was real and to think that I would deliberately hurt my children to bring attention to myself was beyond belief.

I went to see my G.P. and he looked through my medical records. There had never been a diagnosis of Munchausen's Disease. In jest my doctor told me that he could say many things about me but that wouldn't be one of them. He also said that anyone who made that kind of accusation without real proof was nasty and vindictive. I was advised to forget it.

Tom was thrilled with his birthday card and present and I invited him and his daughter to my house for a celebration tea. Then disaster struck. When I opened the fridge a special trifle made for the occasion had degenerated into a soggy mess. By mistake I'd turned the temperature down to zero. Staying calm I phoned Tom asking him to delay his arrival by an hour or so as I had to go into town. I didn't tell him about the trifle. He agreed and I was able to obtain more ingredients and retrieve the situation. The tea was a success, the trifle was delicious and we had a great time just talking and laughing.

At about 8 pm it was time for him to take his daughter home but said that he would return in an hour. Forty minutes later he was knocking at the door. It was 5 weeks into our relationship and this was long enough for both of us to make adult decisions about moving things a stage further. Tom stayed the night; our lovemaking was sensitive and caring. Never before have I felt so wanted and loved. Next morning, before leaving, he said how wonderful it was to sleep next to someone again; I felt the same way and couldn't wait for the next time.

Saturday 8th October 2005

I met up with Tom as usual in the Albert Hotel. He was stood by the karaoke and I went over to him. It was so great to see him and be with him again. The evening was going well until someone, who Tom knows, began roughing up my hair and touching me. I wasn't putting up with that kind of behaviour and told him, politely but firmly, to stop what he was doing. I'm an old fashioned girl and if I am with a man nobody messes around with me. He backed off and we made it through the night with no more interruptions. As usual Tom phoned me later but this time our conversation was different. He was seriously concerned about what had happened earlier. That man's actions had put doubt in his mind about the sort of person I am. I had to promise him that I was his and no one else's. He was insecure, which I could understand and now it is up to me to show him that I mean it when I said that I loved him.

The following evening he was a little late coming into the hotel and I was worried. When he arrived, the other man who had caused the trouble followed him in. It was obvious this man couldn't bear to see us together and he began behaving in an obnoxious way. I tried to ignore him and for most of the time succeeded but he was unable to take "no" for an answer and from the other side of the bar began to say things that a man should not say to a lady. I made him aware how I felt and that he should stop. He signalled across the bar that he thought I'd too much mouth on me. I didn't really care what he thought; I wasn't going to put up with this clown another minute longer and told him so. This infuriated him and he walked over to me, hooked his arm around my neck so I couldn't move my head, then he pressed his face tightly onto mine forcing himself onto me.

I had an immediate flashback to the time when my brother first raped me and I felt sick. I pushed him as hard as I could until he let go, then yelled at him never to do that again. The damage that this man's actions did was incalculable. I was on the phone for over an hour that night trying to reassure Tom that I loved him and that this man was out to make trouble and come between us. When we eventually said goodnight things seemed fine and I told him again that I loved him.

Wednesday 12th October 2005

The comments made about me by my daughters' adoptive mother continue to play on my mind. Dismay turned to anger, where had she obtained the spurious information that I had a serious psychological problem? My only recourse was through legal action, so before consulting a solicitor I asked my doctor for a letter confirming that I did not suffer from Munchausen's Disease. This was readily provided.

I then e-mailed my daughters' adoptive mother asking where the information had come from. I waited two hours for a reply. When it didn't come I telephoned her to check that she had received it. The e-mail had arrived and I asked her to disclose the source of the information. She seemed amused by this and told me quite openly that she had never said these things and that I was making it up. She also said if I started any trouble then I would lose what little contact I had with my daughters.

As well as being slandered, a strong hint of emotional blackmail was now levelled at me. I telephoned my solicitor for an appointment as this had to stop. Earlier, I had phoned Tom, giving him an outline of what was happening. I was concerned about how he would react but he was marvellous, a veritable tower of strength.

Thursday 13th October 2005

I gave my solicitor a full account of what had happened and he said, if proved, this could amount to defamation of character. He continued by saying that if false information had been repeated to others then it would amount to slander. A solicitor's letter to this effect will be sent to my daughters' adoptive mother.

This settled me, I felt more relaxed now that action was being taken and even Tom remarked that I seemed less stressed. I don't think I would have been strong enough to go through with it if it wasn't for him. We settled down to watch the television, there was some football on and we both watched it. Football isn't my game but Tom enjoyed it and I sat beside him absently putting new polish on my fingernails. Then a goal was scored and he jumped off the sofa waving his arms about. He was so excited. It took ages to comb the nail polish out of my hair.

Everything is just perfect, it's as if we have known each other for years.

Friday 14th October 2005

I left him in bed and went downstairs to make some tea. Tom seemed pleased with himself and happy too. Why not, he'd overcome the apprehension of a new relationship, we seemed well suited to each other. At about 10 am he went home and I wandered off into Retford town centre for a look around the shops. All day text messages were passing between us, these are the modern equivalent to love letters and I was "walking on air". Tom will stay the night again, I am positive that everything will go as it did last night. The more time I spend away from him the more I love and miss him.

We talked and watched television until the early hours. Strangely, Tom seemed to have a few nerves again but these disappeared once we were in bed. We had only been asleep for three hours when the phone rang. It was a wrong number but I couldn't get to sleep again. We spent the rest of the day together until 4 pm just "lazing" around. Then he had to go and spend some time with his daughter, and I had to get ready, as we were going to the Albert Hotel later on.

We arrived together and immediately I could sense people looking at us, something was wrong. As the evening progressed only a couple of people spoke to us, the rest either ignored us or made sarcastic remarks. Tom was really quiet and when I asked what was wrong he said it was nothing in particular. I pushed him to tell me but he said I had to wait until Sunday night.

That wasn't good enough; I needed to know what was on his mind. When he eventually told me that he'd been keeping something from me for a while, I began to worry. He said that he was going into hospital next week for an operation. Why hadn't he confided in me? I suppose he had his reasons but I felt hurt. Hopefully it will only be for a 24-hour stay. At home we agreed that the atmosphere in the hotel was awful and I began to cry. I just didn't want to lose the best thing that has ever happened to me. I must be strong for him and learn to cope with situations like that.

Saturday 15th October 2005

Tom was first out of bed and he brought me a drink upstairs. It was wonderful to be pampered. We talked more about his operation and I told him that I would find out the hospital visiting hours. I hate hospitals and I know that he does too. He mentioned that I had been dreaming during the night, I have no recollection of it, but he said it sounded a nice dream. I said it must have been about him. He stayed with me until late in the afternoon and then he had to leave. Tom would be back before my taxi arrived and we could go to the Albert Hotel together. I am dreading being without him but it will be for one night providing all goes well with his surgery. Of more immediate concern was the sort of reception we would get in the hotel that evening.

The disco was playing and we both really enjoyed ourselves. Though we still received a few strange looks from some people the atmosphere was not as strained as during the previous evening. I didn't really care, if people are envious of our happiness that is their problem. Tom asked me how I felt towards him. He already knows, but I reassured him. I think he is more scared than me that we will split up. We spent the night together and I reassured him some more that I loved him.

Sunday 16th October 2005

Tom has the beginnings of a cold, which is something he should avoid right now. It will be 6 weeks tonight since we began going out together and it still feels as wonderful as ever. My feelings are so strong that I would move a mountain just to be with him. We are going to the Albert Hotel again tonight so I hope all goes well.

The atmosphere in the hotel was tense so we just laughed and joked between ourselves. However, I was affected by it and it showed. Tom said there was something he wanted to ask me but it would wait. The

D.J. came across and began talking to us. I told him that Tom wanted to ask me something and he said he knew what it was but asked if we could leave it until Saturday night when it could be announced from the stage. I was really puzzled about this, what could it be? Considering the attitude of other people towards us I wondered about the wisdom of announcing anything personal from the stage. Anyhow, time will tell.

Monday 17th October 2005

Today was yet another milestone in our relationship. We walked hand in hand through Retford town centre and I felt so proud. It was 13 years since I'd had a man on my arm and it felt fantastic. Although he hadn't mentioned marriage, Tom asked if we could become engaged. His quietness the previous evening must have been related to this, he was probably plucking up courage or just biding his time. Anyway, I said yes and my heart sang. That evening, Tom brought his daughter back to my house for an evening meal. Everything turned out well, the food, the amount I cooked, and I wasn't in the slightest bit nervous. I suppose she is the sort of daughter I never had, as my own wouldn't give me a chance.

Thursday 20th October 2005

The post arrived. It contained a copy of the solicitor's letter sent to my daughters' adopted mother. The wording was delicate yet stern, which I was pleased about. Hopefully there would be no more false accusations from that direction.

After lunch Tom collected me and we went into town to choose an engagement ring. The jeweller had so many that I was spoilt for choice but there was one that caught my eye. I tried it on several times; it was my favourite stone, blue topaz, with diamonds surrounding it, I'd never seen such a beautiful ring. This was the one, I couldn't stop laughing and the girls that served us said I was getting emotional. Well, it's not every day a girl gets engaged.

We now had the ring but he hadn't yet asked me to marry him. Then he dropped to one knee, something no other man has ever done to me, and said,

"Rose, will you marry me?"

"Yes, of course I will marry you," I replied.

We kissed and cuddled and then he had to go, but I knew it would only be a short time before he returned for the evening. In the meantime, I had a beautiful ring to remind me of him. There was no turning back now.

Saturday 22nd October 2005

Tom said he wanted our engagement to be announced at the Albert Hotel when he would formally place the ring on my finger. That's what all the secrecy was about last Sunday. He was nervous all day but I think my nerves will show when the time comes for me to stand on the stage. I know, in Tom, I've found a treasure. He is a wonderful, precious man. We understand each other, we have both been hurt through relationships that have gone wrong but this was the real thing. I wondered how people would react, it had been kept low key and we felt the need to get engaged to prove to others and ourselves just how we feel about each other. I was still a bit concerned that some people would be envious and spoil the evening.

The Albert Hotel was full and I had a quiet word with the D.J. about how I wanted it all planned. I couldn't resist showing him my engagement ring, which was in my handbag. I also showed it to his fiancée, who I knew could keep a secret.

I asked Tom if we could wait for the gentleman who said he knew my dad and who always spoke well of him. Tom agreed but had a puzzled look. The gentleman came in and I asked him to follow me to the back of the hotel where I showed him my engagement ring. I explained what would be happening and there was something important I had to ask him. Although the date for our wedding had not been finalised, I wanted this gentleman to stand by my side in place of my late father. To my delight he said he would do anything for me.

We were invited onto the stage and the D.J. instructed Tom to get on one knee, which I begged him not to do as he'd already done that at home. Poor Tom was a nervous wreck. He placed the ring on my finger and mumbled his thanks to the audience. I thanked everyone and made a short speech in which I told people of the wonderful gesture made by my father's old friend.

The D.J. played "Don't close your eyes", "Let it be me," "Dream" and "I don't know much but I know I love you". Compared with previous evenings, it was a different atmosphere altogether, people were kind and wished us well. The evening was special and one of the female bar staff sang "Crazy", which just about summed up how I felt.

Saturday 29th October 2005

All week Tom has been acting completely out of character, it is too difficult to fully explain but I am gaining the impression that he is unsure that our relationship is strong enough to last. I am hoping for a simpler explanation but the constant need to reassure him is exhausting me. It is becoming a serious problem for me and things would have to improve, otherwise the future would be uncertain.

Sunday 30th October 2005

People in the Albert Hotel must have noticed how cool things were between us. I had chosen to end our relationship but hadn't yet told him. I was dreading it, but I was not happy and he had to be told. I needed someone trustworthy to talk with so I discussed my decision with the landlord. He'd always stood by me in the past but today he said I was "out of order" and should think of Tom and what this would do to him. Later, at home I knew I didn't feel the same about him any longer but still could not find the courage to tell him. I could tell by his questions that he knew; my engagement ring was returned to its box.

Monday 31st October 2005

Tom had stayed the night but nothing happened between us and I slept fitfully.

For most of the morning I fretted about what to do for the best. I knew that if it was over then I had to say so sooner rather than later. I couldn't pretend things were alright when they weren't as that would be very wrong of me. Eventually I made a decision and locked the doors and windows then sent Tom a text message telling him that I couldn't carry on seeing him.

I knew what his reaction would be, so I went upstairs and shut myself in the bedroom. Within minutes he was around at my house and I was pleased that I had the sense to lock my door. He was very angry and hammered on the door, but I ignored him. Then my mobile phone rang, he asked me what was wrong, I told him that it was my fault not his. I said that I had gone into town, which was a lie but I didn't want him making a scene at my front door.

He wanted an explanation, why had I suddenly gone off him, what had he done wrong? All I could say was that we had moved too quickly, we had become engaged without getting to know each other properly. He wanted to know if I would be going to the Albert Hotel that night, but how could I, it would be like rubbing salt into his wounds. It wasn't easy for me to end our relationship but I couldn't lead him on and then lie about it. I spoke to his daughter on the phone and said how sorry I was and tried to explain that everything had been too quick. She agreed with me. I said that should her dad get too drunk that night and she needed my help, she only had to call, as he told me he would be doing just that. I did say that we could remain friends.

Tuesday 1st November 2005

Tom phoned to ask if he could pick up a few of his belongings but I was more interested in how people had reacted in the Albert Hotel when he turned up on his own. I decided to go to the Albert Hotel that evening and face the sarcastic remarks and looks of disbelief that I knew would come my way. Tom was there and we behaved in a civilised way towards each other but the atmosphere was hostile. I sang a few songs at the karaoke but began to feel unwell. The lyrics were not fluent, my brain began to slow down and I knew a fit was coming on.

In slurred speech I asked Tom to get some help from one of my friends who was sat across the room from us. I had to get out of the main room; the indignity of having an epileptic seizure in front of other people was something I wanted to avoid. We managed to reach the toilets after which I remembered no more until coming round on the floor. I had no idea how long the fit had lasted, I felt so ill afterwards. When I had recovered enough to return to the main room the friend who had helped bought me a drink and I sat with her for a while. When I was sure that I had sufficiently recovered enough to move about on my own I sat at the bar with Tom, but still felt really ill. It seemed an age before my taxi arrived but when it did, Tom asked if he could get a lift home. When he was dropped off I asked him to telephone me the following day.

Wednesday 2nd November 2005

It was late afternoon when Tom rang. I'd been resting and was still aching from the seizure, it must have been a bad one for the effects to have lasted this long. He asked how I was, there wasn't much of a conversation but he told me that he'd be in the Albert Hotel at the weekend and hoped to see me there. I said it would be better for everyone concerned if I found somewhere else to go. He then rang off. I thought long and hard before sending him a text message asking if he'd made any plans for that night, if not would he like to talk things through. I received a reply asking me whether I meant on the phone or for him to come to my house. Well, I saw the funny side of it and invited him round.

It was strange to hear him knock at the door, especially as he had a key. We didn't talk much about our relationship but remained open with each other whilst discussing other things. In time we broached the subject of where we stood as a couple and decided to give it another try, but not to rush things this time. I phoned his daughter and she was so pleased, she really is a lovely girl.

Friday 4ᵗʰ November 2005

Our relationship is back on track, which pleased me. Tonight would be the first time I'd been to the Albert Hotel for a week. I asked Tom to meet me in the foyer because by the time I arrived he would have judged the mood inside the hotel. I instructed the taxi driver to wait until I'd received reassurance that my presence there would not cause problems for Tom. He met me at the door and said things were fine and there was nothing to worry about, so I told the taxi driver to go and then followed Tom into the hotel bar.

I could sense people looking at me but I suppose I half expected that, anyway in a few weeks time they would find someone else to talk about. The landlord was still a bit hostile towards me, he repeated that I was out of order but it wasn't his relationship and at least we hadn't been arguing in the hotel or causing trouble.

Saturday 5ᵗʰ November 2005

The landlord still had to have his say tonight when Tom and I went to the Albert Hotel, but he had softened and we enjoyed the evening. Things seemed to be returning to normal.

Sunday 6th November 2005

We decided to stay away from the Albert Hotel today so I invited Tom and his daughter for Sunday lunch. The vegetables were prepared the night before and I put the beef into roast at around 10.30 am. They arrived at about 2 pm and everything was ready except for the Yorkshire puddings – these would be cooked last of all. I love making Yorkshire puddings from the mix. Pre-made ones never taste quite like those you make yourself. I was hoping and praying they would turn out well. I poured the mix into a baking tray and put it into the oven, which was set at the correct temperature. I went back and forth to the oven door trying to see what was happening by the flickering glow of my cigarette lighter, as I knew that if I opened the door my puddings would collapse.

When everything else had been served onto plates I took my Yorkshire puddings from the oven. They had risen so much that I felt like putting scaffolding round them – they were truly majestic, these were puddings that were far too good to eat. Tom's daughter was amazed; the expression on her face said it all.

Usually if I am under pressure or worried then nothing goes to plan but there was nothing to worry about today and a good time was had by all. Tom asked what we would say to people at the Albert Hotel if they asked why we hadn't been in that night. My cryptic answer was to say that we had a prior engagement. Tom just looked puzzled.

Monday 7th November 2005

It was mid morning when I took my engagement ring from it's box and passed it to Tom. I said that this was the prior engagement I had spoken about the previous evening. For the second time he placed the ring on my finger, then together we phoned his daughter with the news. She appeared relieved but I could sense in her voice that she still had some reservations; perhaps she was concerned that her father would be hurt yet again.

Tuesday 8th November 2005

I'd been building up to something all day and by early evening I was feeling deeply depressed. My mood was such that when Tom asked what was wrong I began to cry. Daniel was in my head and even after all this time I am still grieving for him. Until I fully accept that he is dead I will always have days when I feel utterly dejected and lost.

Wednesday 9th November 2005

My mood had lightened today and Tom remarked how nice it was to see me smile again.

Thursday 10th November 2005

Today I had a surprise in store for Tom. I asked him to come shopping with me. To my surprise he agreed, but I wasn't so sure that he would enjoy it very much. It turned out to be a great day, we laughed as we walked round Retford's shops and discovered many new things about each other. Normally, men hate shopping but this was a change of scenery for Tom, which he seemed to enjoy. It was an experience for both of us.

Friday 11th November 2005

As usual, we were in the Albert Hotel when something strange happened. Whilst we stood at the bar the man who had said that he knew my dad began to come on strong. He put his arm around me, which to begin with I didn't mind; it just seemed like a friendly gesture. He then whispered that it was a shame that Tom was there too. I was shocked and pushed him away. Tom was unaware of what had happened and for the rest of the evening I tried to act normally. It wasn't until we arrived home that I mentioned it to Tom. Even then, I didn't tell him the whole story, particularly about the comment that had been made regarding Tom's presence.

I had serious reservations that this man may not have known my dad at all. For a start, he was quite a lot younger than my dad would have been had he lived.

Saturday 12th November 2005

I talked to the man about my dad again, I asked the sort of questions that only someone who had know him well could have answered. This man had no idea what I was talking about.

Tuesday 15th November 2005

I have an old photograph of my brother, his wife and their baby son, which I took to the hotel. I produced the photo and asked the man to tell me who it was. Immediately, he said it was my dad yet my brother resembles my mother. Anyone who had known my dad would not have made that mistake. My anger began to show. How could anyone be so cruel? It was clear that he thought he could take advantage of my trust.

Monday 21st November 2005

I remember Tom getting out of bed and going downstairs to make the tea. I also remember telling him that I would be down soon, as I had a lot to do and I wanted an early start to the day. However, that was all I remembered until I regained consciousness. Tom had come back upstairs and I was evidently laid under the bed. He had heard 2 loud bangs on the bedroom floor and came to investigate. I had had a seizure and collapsed. Although Tom knew about my epilepsy and what to do when I have a fit, it must still be a shock when it happens. He laid me on my side and made sure that

I could breathe. Then he stayed with me until I came round.

Afterwards I hurt everywhere, because during a fit my entire body goes into spasm. Despite the discomfort I have to stay active and for the rest of the day I never stopped, I was looking for things to do to keep me busy and on my feet. By the end of the day I was exhausted; all I wanted to do was sleep. I made an appointment with my G.P. for tomorrow, as I wanted reassurance that no damage had been done to my head.

Tuesday 22nd November 2005

Tom waited patiently in the waiting room whilst I saw the doctor, who told me that I had concussion. I mentioned to the doctor that I had a new partner and it must have been a shock for him to see me convulsing like that. He shook Tom's hand and told him what was wrong with me to put his mind at ease. Tom has been extremely supportive through all of this and I am so grateful.

CHAPTER SEVEN ────────────────

Monday 28th November 2005

Things are going well between Tom and me and I am now more certain than ever that this is what I want. Whilst he stays with me as a guest for most of the time now, Tom still has his own home to run and needs to spend time there with his daughter.

Everywhere this week has had snow and gale force winds except Retford, until today. Just as we set foot outside to go into town it began to snow. I love to watch snow as it settles on the lawn, seeing it brings back some of my happier childhood memories of playing snowballs and building snowmen in the field next to the farm cottage where I used to live. However, I'm not too thrilled about going shopping in it.

Thursday 1ˢᵗ December 2005

Normally, I would have decorated my Christmas tree yesterday but I was too tired so I set about doing it today. Tom looked on as I hung each bauble with precision. It had to be perfect with nothing out of place. As the tree took shape I began to feel some sadness. Daniel would be watching, and knowing that I had done something that he loved meant everything to me. Decorating the tree can take up to 3 hours but I carried on until it was finished. Tom kept me going with cups of tea. When it was finished I stood back to admire my handiwork. A few adjustments here and there and I was happy with it.

Friday 2ⁿᵈ December 2005

As Christmas was approaching I decided to telephone Mrs Warburton whose husband ran the farm where I had spent my early childhood. I wanted to deliver her card in person. She was always kind to me and thought very highly of my dad who worked on the farm. I told her about Tom and that we were engaged. She was genuinely delighted as she knew the story of my life and wanted only happiness for me. Mrs Warburton suggested we join her for morning coffee on a day nearer Christmas. I really can't wait to see the old place again; just hearing Mrs Warburton's voice again brought back so many great memories for me.

Saturday 3rd December 2005

For no apparent reason, whilst we were watching television, one of the ornaments flew off the top of the television. It didn't even slide off; it flew into the air before hitting the floor. We were stunned by this and felt very uncomfortable. Even the leaves on a nearby plant were moving; it had taken some kind of force to make this happen.

I telephoned Michael at the Spiritualist Church hoping he could come up with some ideas. He suggested that I take a firm line with whatever was doing this. Michael said that I had to be stern and tell it to leave us alone. I was sure it wasn't Daniel's spirit because he would never do things like that to alarm me. Tom said that if he hadn't seen it for himself he wouldn't have believed it. I felt the same. Anyway, a strong word or two from me did the trick and there was no repetition of the bizarre happening. I was pleased about this because some of my ornaments are very dear to me.

Putting this behind us we went to the Albert Hotel. Tom was quiet all evening, hardly saying a word. Later, at home, I asked what was wrong. Tom became agitated; he mentioned that a person at the bar had been asking him questions about me. My immediate reaction was to be inquisitive; I wanted to know what the questions were. When he told me I became angry. The person began by asking if everything was alright between us both, which I suppose was not too intrusive. Then Tom was asked if I'd tried to "rip him off". Now that was totally out of order and I was standing for none of it. I couldn't let the subject drop but Tom wouldn't tell me who it was asking the questions.

Sunday 4th December 2005

I began thinking of a way to get to the bottom of it and discover who the culprit was. Tom knew he would have to face me again. I couldn't understand why he wouldn't name the person, particularly as he said that the questions were asked in a general way without any nastiness. As the hours passed by I became increasingly angry. Tom realised he couldn't win; he had to name the culprit. To force his hand I phoned John, my ex-partner, to ask him to tell Tom that in the 10 years that I had known him, not once had I tried to "rip him off". This shocked Tom into telling me who it was. The name he gave me came as a shock. To make matters worse it was a man who I had some regard for, but not anymore. He had even told Tom that he was "looking out for him". I'm certain that Tom is old enough to look out for himself.

From this disagreeable episode came a realisation that if I get even a hint of someone insinuating untruths about me I will pursue the matter doggedly. Tom said that I'd exhausted him; maybe if I hadn't threatened to telephone John he would still be having his ears pinned back.

Tuesday 6th December 2005

Today Tom was admitted into the local hospital for an exploratory operation. Although the surgery went well, he still had to have continuing treatment to ensure that cancer wasn't present. All day I missed him like crazy and was very worried. His daughter had gone to the hospital with him and stayed there all day. I visited in the evening. It seemed strange to see him in a hospital bed; he looked weak and frail. The plan was for him to return to his own home the following day but it would be unfair to expect his daughter to carry the full burden of his care. I said that when he felt up to it he should come to my house and I would look after him.

Thursday 8th December 2005

Tom could barely walk when he came through my front door; he looked so poorly. The house was warm and I settled him into an armchair. He was obviously sore and tender but the pain was under control and bearable.

Saturday 10th December 2005

Over the past few days Tom has begun to regain his strength, I'd always wanted to be a nurse, perhaps I should have been because I quite enjoyed looking after him.

Tom's daughter is becoming more independent, which was a good thing. Now when she wants to see her dad, she orders a taxi, stays for tea then later goes home on her own.

Sunday 11th December 2005

Tom began to pass blood clots in his urine. It didn't worry him as much as it did me, he said that some bleeding was quite normal following the kind of operation he'd had. I was not convinced particularly as the pain had returned and was causing him great discomfort. His appetite disappeared and I had to beg him to eat something to keep his strength up.

Tuesday 13th December 2005

Over the past day or two things have worsened, neither of us are getting much sleep.

The pain seems to be worse at night; at times it was more than he could bear and he would go downstairs so as not to wake me. It would only be when I turned over that I realised he wasn't there. He would be laid on the couch in agony.

Wednesday 14th December 2005

By now Tom was vomiting so against his wishes I called the doctor's surgery. I explained what was happening and the doctor said he would visit as soon as he could. The weekly shopping trip could wait, as Tom was my first priority. The doctor examined Tom and diagnosed a severe kidney infection. He prescribed a course of strong antibiotics and told Tom not to expect any immediate relief. I collected the tablets and the pharmacist said the same thing, it would be 24 hours before any signs of improvement would be seen. By now he'd lost a lot of weight, he was quite a slight person to begin with, now Tom looked positively emaciated. However, I made it my duty to look after him and restore him to his previous good health.

Saturday 17th December 2005

During the past week I'd wrapped Christmas gifts for our friends. Tom was improving and his sense of humour had returned. Today he went into Retford with his daughter. Although they enjoyed each other's company, Tom was very tired when he returned; I hoped he hadn't overdone it. I needn't have worried as the fresh air and exercise had been good for him. It also gave his daughter a chance to spend some quality time with her dad. Being the thoughtful man he is, Tom had bought a floral tribute to Daniel; we will place it on his grave on Monday.

After resting for an hour or two Tom appeared well enough to go out so in the evening we went to the Albert Hotel. Everyone was pleased to see us, they wondered where we had been and when we explained that Tom had been in hospital they were so supportive. However, after a while, Tom began to wilt, he looked grey and worn out. I called a taxi and took him home. He said that he'd enjoyed the evening but would have to take things easy for a while longer. The kidney infection had taken more out of him than we both realised.

Monday 19th December 2005

Today we did some last minute Christmas shopping. This was the first time we had been in town together since Tom came out of hospital and even though it was grey and overcast it felt wonderful just walking around the shops with him. However, it was a day of mixed emotions as, together, we visited Daniel's grave to clean his headstone and leave the wreath that Tom had bought. It was upsetting, it always is, but these are the things a mother has to do and I like his grave to look cared for. In life he was always a smart boy and his grave must always reflect that aspect of his life.

Over the past few days I've been feeling low but put it down to the time of year. There may be some truth in certain people being affected by dark cold winter days, perhaps I am one of them. I tried hard not to let my inner feelings show too much, this must have been successful because people remarked on how happy I looked. I guess this is down to Tom; he makes me feel so special.

Thursday 22nd December 2005

Not long now before Christmas comes and goes. Today, as usual, I go shopping and this week Tom was well enough to come with me. We were walking through town when a lady beckoned to us. I knew straight away who she was but Tom didn't. She was a gypsy lady and call me superstitious but I never ignore a gypsy. She told us both a lot of things all of which were true. Then she asked if we would buy a lucky charm. I chose holly with berries on it and Tom chose a lucky stone, he was so pleased with what had happened. We called into Clair's shop to wish her a Happy Christmas. She gave me a hug and hoped that we would have a good holiday too.

Tomorrow night we'll be going to the Albert Hotel, we haven't been out much lately so I'm looking forward to meeting up with friends again and singing a few songs. All the Christmas food is in the fridge so I don't think we'll go short of anything, I'm looking forward to a happy, relaxed weekend.

Friday 23rd December 2005

The Albert Hotel was full. I must have sung at least 6 songs and thought they all went quite well, until I sang "When you tell me that you love me". The last person I expect criticism from is Tom so I felt insulted when he remarked that I had sung it far too high; I was fuming, what did he know about singing anyway? I ignored him and sang another song called "I believe". A young man stood behind me said how well I was doing and then began to sing at the top of his voice; I couldn't hear myself, which for a singer is not good. Once the song had ended I advised him not to do that again when I was singing. I was polite but firm. The man who runs the karaoke agreed that he should not have done what he did.

Then, yet again, Tom surprised me. He told me not to cause any trouble, as he couldn't back me up in his condition. It seems that he is still to learn that if I have a problem with anything I deal with it myself and don't need back up. For the remainder of the evening things were a bit frosty between us.

Christmas Eve 2005

Tom had already suggested that we stay at home; he said he couldn't stand the crowds and noise. He didn't fool me because I know that he can be jealous should anyone approach me, so imagine his reaction to other men wishing me a Happy Christmas with a kiss. I gave in to him and we spent the evening at home. It was so boring; we were practically looking for things to do. For an extrovert like me Christmas Eve should be spent in the pub not at home, but Tom wanted a quiet night in front of the television and that is what he got.

Christmas Day 2005

Today, I shed a few tears for Daniel who was very much a "Christmas person"; he loved everything about it. Tom collected his daughter and we enjoyed Christmas lunch together. She stayed all day until quite late, which made a pleasant change. She liked the gifts that I had bought her; anyway I have to spoil someone now that Daniel is no longer here. It was a pleasant, satisfying day but at about 8 pm I fell asleep for a short time and Tom took his daughter home. When I awoke he had not yet returned so I just gazed at the tree and relived the happy times when Daniel and my other children were small and still believed in Santa Claus. I have to watch myself though, in case I get too maudlin.

Boxing Day 2005

Today was easier to manage. The turkey, already cooked from the day before, just needed cutting up. Generally, we took it easy but when it came to washing the dishes Tom thought that his daughter would be helping me. What a shock to his male ego when I asked him to do them. I'd done all the cooking and wanted to watch a film on television. Tom realised that he had to do his share of the chores, especially if he wants to be involved with me on a long-term basis. Washing up exhausted the poor man so he needs more practice, which I will arrange for him.

Friday 30th December 2005

By the end of the week following Christmas things were back to normal. It was just a case of going shopping to get everything for the New Year. A large joint of beef is already in the freezer; all we needed was fresh vegetables and the usual weekly food.

New Years Eve 2005

Standing room only in the Albert Hotel. Many of the revellers were strangers and as intoxication increased so did the noise level. By the time it reached the witching hour the din was deafening but it was all good humoured. Tom had agreed to drive because taxis were at a premium. Because of this he could not drink but that didn't seem to bother him, he remained mildly amused at some of the antics going on around him.

New Years Day 2006

It was 2 am and we were still in the Albert Hotel. No one seemed to want to leave but I knew I had to be up and about earlier than usual so reluctantly we went home. Tom's daughter was coming for dinner again so I had to make sure everything was just right. Everything went to plan which made me even more confident. Not that I am a bad cook, but I just don't like things to turn out wrong. The whole day was a total success, but come the early evening I was shattered.

CHAPTER EIGHT ────────────────

A new year has begun and more than ever I must move on with my life. On the 3rd of January Tom was booked to go for a check up with the consultant who performed his operation. He was apprehensive that morning as anyone would be. On his return the look of relief on his face said it all. He'd been given the all clear, so he can get on with his life as well.

Friday 6th January 2006

Earlier in 2005 I had contacted the Trisha show on television. It was when my first book had been published and I wanted to help others who had suffered the same experiences in their lives as I had. Today I received a telephone call from a lady who told me that she was a researcher on the Trisha show. She asked several questions about my life and the book and told me that she would be speaking to her producer and would contact me again in the afternoon. During the time

I was speaking with her, Tom was in the living room wondering what was going on. I don't think he believed me when I told him who it was that had called.

After lunch I did some ironing to keep busy and whispered to Daniel that if he should be watching please let this be my big break. Then one of my ornamental dolls fell onto its face. When I stood it back up it was as if I could sense Daniel in the room. A few minutes later my phone rang; it was the researcher from the Trisha show. I'd not held out much hope that she would get back to me so when she did I was quite surprised. She said that her producer was definitely interested and I was being considered for a show dealing with abuse. She couldn't give a specific date but it would be on a Friday and I would have to travel to the studios in London. She said someone from the show would call me again next week with the date.

I was amazed. I rang Tom and both he and his daughter were pleased for me. Then I called Clair and told her, she was really excited. I told my publisher what had happened and he was pleased. I think he was a little cautious about it but wished me well. All I have to do now is wait until the researcher lets me know the date of the show.

Monday 9th January 2006

Tom and me went into town to do some shopping. Before long I was telling everyone that I knew about my possible appearance on the Trisha show. I went into my local newspaper office where I have good contacts. All my details were taken and I was told that someone would contact me about it.

Tuesday 10th January 2006

I had not long finished breakfast, my hair wasn't washed and my face was still in its jar, when the phone rang. The newspaper wanted some pictures and a photographer would be round in approximately an hour's time. I stammered that I hadn't got my make up on yet, though I was ready when he arrived. He took a lot of pictures; this was a big story for them just as it was exciting for me. All I could do now was wait for Trisha's researchers to contact me with a date for the show.

Thursday 12th January 2006

As usual I went into town to do my weekly shop. Tom was with me and we called in at the newspaper office to collect copies of the edition that I hoped would carry the story. The office was closed but Tom said he would collect a few copies later in the day. I phoned the newspaper office to make certain that it was is this week's edition. The receptionist said it was and assured me that the article did me credit. When I saw the headlines "Retford Woman Appears On Trisha" I was stunned. It now felt as though it was actually happening. Tom's daughter remarked that my 15 minutes of fame was on the way.

Monday 16th January 2005

I waited expectantly for a call from the television researchers, but by 4 pm nothing had happened, so I called them. I spoke to the same researcher who had dealt with me from the beginning. She said the show would be recorded on the 17th of February. It was then I probably made an error of judgment because I began to say more about my brother and how my mother had encouraged him to sexually abuse me. I remarked that once my father had died when I was 8 years of age my mother had become a bitter and twisted woman. I also informed her about the newspaper article and she asked me to send her a copy. I was given assurance that the programme would keep me updated. As well as the Trisha show there was something else occupying my mind.

Thursday 19th January 2006

I think I may be pregnant. Normally I would have been pleased but because of my age and my epilepsy, I felt concerned. A pregnancy testing kit reassured me that I wasn't having a baby but all the symptoms were there and I wouldn't be satisfied until my doctor had confirmed things one way or the other.

Saturday 21st January 2006

We were in the Albert Hotel when I noticed that Tom was drinking much more than he usually did. I mentioned that he should space his drinks out and he reassured me that he would. However, not long into the evening, he asked me a question that took me completely by surprise.

"Have you been with anyone else since I've been with you?" he asked.

I didn't know where to look and told him not to think such things. I wanted to know what lay behind his question. He told me he thought that he might have picked something up from sleeping with me. He was drunk and talking nonsense. I was angry and said to wait until we got home where we could discuss it in private.

Once inside my front door I demanded proof of his allegation. I wanted to know why Tom thought he'd caught something from me, but he remained silent. Rather than start a full blown argument I calmly unlocked the back door and told him to leave. He asked how he was supposed to get home, as he could not drive with all that drink in his system. I told him to walk home. He picked up his keys and left quietly. I locked the door and went to bed where I hardly slept. What Tom had said was hateful and hurtful; I am not a person who sleeps around and he knows it.

Sunday 22nd January 2006

I left it until the afternoon before trying to call Tom. There was no reply the first time but when I tried again later he answered the phone. Calmly I inquired when he planned to collect his belongings, he gave some idea of what time he would arrive. Because his car was still parked outside my house he had to walk. When he finally arrived I made us both a hot drink. It was a cold day and the heating had been on for several hours so the house was warm and cosy. Tom's face was pinched; he looked half frozen. I invited him to sit down and when the hot drink began to have an effect we began to talk. Tom knew what he'd said the previous evening was totally wrong, he told me that it was the drink talking. I always try to give people the benefit of the doubt but I remained uncertain. However, he did seem to be genuinely sorry so I let him stay.

Monday 30th January 2006

Things are going smoothly again, but I think he understands what would happen if ever there was a next time. Just after lunch I phoned the Tricia researcher to inquire about progress. I was stunned when she said that the programme had been rescheduled for recording on Friday 3rd February and not the 17th. This seemed very odd because had I not taken it upon myself to phone them, how would I have known?

I was told that she would call again at 4 pm, which she did. She asked lots of questions about my life and different things that had happened over the years. This lasted for about an hour and before ringing off she said she would call again tomorrow for another chat. I felt quite proud of what I had achieved lately and I knew that Daniel would be proud of me too.

Tuesday 31st January 2006

Just prior to lunch I realised that I'd missed a call on my mobile phone. It was from the television company, so I called them. I was told the researcher would contact me in the next few minutes. She requested contact numbers for my daughters and son and when I said I couldn't do that she didn't seem to mind and said that it wouldn't affect the show going ahead. This bothered me, why would the programme need to involve my children, surely the reason for putting me on the show was to talk about my experiences, not theirs. Then she asked for my sisters' telephone numbers, again I refused.

I was told she would call me later in the afternoon to see if I had changed my mind. In between time I called my son's foster parent and asked what his reaction had been to all the press coverage I'd received, particularly as I may be appearing on television. She said he wasn't pleased and couldn't understand why I needed all this publicity. I explained that I wanted my book to go further and there wasn't much my son could do about it.

Later, when I spoke to the researcher again I was informed that the producer wanted to ask me further questions. This proved to be a painful exercise as his questions brought back memories that I had locked away many years ago. It seemed odd that none of his questions were connected to the abuse that I had suffered but were all about my children. He asked whether I considered myself to be a bad mother and if I had ever abused my children. He received an emphatic "no" to both questions. He tried his best to get contact numbers from me, but I wouldn't give them to him. Then he politely told me that there was no way that I could appear on the show. I said "OK" and put the phone down.

I was numb, I felt cold, angry and gutted. Not only that, I felt humiliated. When I began to cry just to let the anger I found I couldn't stop, the tears just kept coming. I called my local newspaper and asked them if they wanted a real story they could have one. I was quite prepared to say what I thought about the way I'd been treated by the television company. After my experience I think people should be aware of T.V. researchers and the way they pry into people's personal lives and the questions they ask. Some may say that's their job but it caused me considerable pain, especially as it brought back all the horrible memories of when I gave my children up for adoption.

Wednesday 1st February 2006

I decided to telephone the complaints department at the Trisha show. I made it quite clear to the lady that I spoke to how unhappy I was with the way the producer had asked me nasty and vindictive questions regarding my children. I said that it was my understanding that my appearance on the show was to tell my story of how I had been abused and raped by my brother. How wrong could I have been? I was told bluntly that the show was all about helping families and that they needed my children on the show with me. Again I refused to give any details of their whereabouts. My children are fully aware of the abuse I had suffered but this was supposed to be about my life, not theirs. The real horror, if I had gone ahead with the show, would have been for my brother to appear. It is unlikely, had that happened, that I would have stayed in control of my temper. This was a narrow escape, the thought of being tortured all over again kept me awake for the rest of the week.

Saturday 4th February 2006

I lay in bed thinking it would have been today in 1969 that my dad passed away. There are times when I feel the awful sadness of losing a dad that I loved so much. I am certain that had he not died when he did, my life would have been much happier. I wouldn't have had to live a life of hell at the hands of my mother and brother; he would have stopped that happening.

Tuesday 8th February 2006

It's a bit early for Spring-cleaning but I decided to make a start on my kitchen. This entailed washing the net curtains, scrubbing the lights and re-painting an entire wall. Tom did all the scrubbing and I got on with the rest of the work. When I was only 10 years old my mother made me do the decorating, scrubbing and cleaning, which should have put me off it for life. However, it seemed to have the opposite effect and I thoroughly enjoy keeping my home neat and tidy; in fact I'm almost obsessional about it.

The kitchen took about 6 hours to redecorate and towards the end I noticed that one of the door frames needed to be scrubbed. Tom suggested that we left it until the following day but I said it would be better to finish the whole job off at one go. It was then I saw paint on his jumper and I had to scrub that as well. For some reason Tom's reaction to this amused me and I began to laugh. Turning away from him my arm knocked a pot mouse ornament from a stool, smashing one of its ears. By now I was laughing so much that I had to run upstairs to control myself. I have never known such a small job cause so much trouble.

I'd just composed myself when the local newspaper phoned regarding my non-appearance on the Trisha show. I explained to the reporter what had happened and he told me that he would try to put an article in the next edition of the paper. One of the walls had dried patchy and would have to be repainted – this could wait until tomorrow. Oh, by the way I forgot to mention, I'm not pregnant.

CHAPTER NINE ─────────────

O nce again I'm feeling uncertain about my
relationship with Tom. My life has always been
one of uncertainties and as each day passes I become
more convinced that I would be better off living on my
own. Although Tom treats me well he is quite possessive
and the only part of the week I enjoy is my shopping day
on a Thursday. I tell myself that I can't let this situation
carry on for much longer. One of my close friends has
told me to end it but sometimes it's easier said than
done. The longer I leave it, the harder it will become to
finish with him.

Thursday 9th February 2006

It's shopping day and Tom is with me. Our walk around
the Retford town centre shops has gone well and, as
usual, I enjoyed myself. Tom seemed happy enough
to trek around with me. It's when we arrive home that
things change. Apart from going to the Albert Hotel

at weekends we never seem to go anywhere else. I am beginning to feel hemmed in. People may think that I'm cruel and selfish but that isn't the issue at all. I am tired of going to town only once a week instead of maybe 2 or 3 times. We haven't been to the Albert Hotel for a couple of weeks now, but when we are there Tom regularly "puts me down" about one thing or another. Should I have an innocent conversation with another man, or even if men speak to me, he becomes annoyed and accuses me of things I haven't done.

Friday 10th February 2006

Tom wanted to stay in but I said that wasn't an option, Fridays are usually quite good at the Albert Hotel and another night in front of the television would drive me mad. The karaoke was in full swing and everything was going well until around 10.30 pm. There is a man who sings really well and when it's his turn everyone in the hotel applauds and encourages him. Tom took exception when I shouted with the other people and said that for all he knew I was another notch on this man's bedpost. Well, I'm afraid that was the last straw. I knew what I had to do; it was just a question of when and how. My timing had to be perfect.

I remained calm and cool until we arrived back home, then I questioned him about the evening. He tried to deny everything, but I was the one who had been on soft drinks all night and knew exactly what had been said and in what context. We talked things over and not wishing to throw him out at such a late hour I permitted him to stay the night. In the morning I asked him again why he was behaving in such an unreasonable way. His actions were driving a wedge between us. He didn't have an answer except perhaps it was the drink that made him say such things.

It was mid morning when I received a phone call from my publisher who told me that a bookshop in Grimsby was stocking my book "More than I Deserved". Naturally I was pleased, but as for celebrating, that was definitely not at the top of my list. Tom asked me several times what I wanted to do and I had to tell him that I needed space and time to decide. He asked if I wanted him there whilst I did this but I told him to go. I felt no emotion as he packed his clothes and other belongings. He said that he didn't know what he was going to tell his daughter, I advised him to tell her the truth. He should tell her that I couldn't live a life where someone is trying to control me. I'd lived that kind of life once before and now I am old enough and wise enough to say "no" that is exactly what I mean.

Tom asked me if I was certain that this was what I wanted and I said it was. As he had already taken his belongings to the car, all that was left to do was say our goodbyes. I felt a bit sorry for him but a relationship has to be based on trust otherwise it will fail. As the door closed behind him I felt a huge weight lift from my shoulders. Once again I was my own person; the old

Rosie was back, I felt so different inside. Above all, my house was my own again.

Wednesday 15th February 2006

John the taxi driver has reappeared. He called to say that he couldn't go to work as he had the flu. I hadn't anything particularly special to do that day so I decided to go round to his house and help him out. I cooked a few meals and that way at least I knew he would have some decent food inside him. I stayed until around 7 pm but as I'd left one of my windows open I had to go home. Even though my neighbour would keep a watch on things I couldn't take any chances of being burgled. Anyway, Alfie was ill so that was another reason for going home.

Later, I sent a text message to Tom. I felt that I hadn't said goodbye properly and asked him to call me, which he did. On the phone we managed to stay civil to each other and after a brief conversation we finally said our goodbyes. I felt much better.

Thursday 16th February 2006

Shopping day and as I was going into town I phoned John to inquire how he was. He was considering going back to work but still felt ill. I said I thought that was unwise. He called me back to say that another driver had agreed to cover for him. After I had done my shopping I went to see him, perhaps this wasn't necessary but that is the kind of person I am. Sometimes I wonder who will take care of me when I need help.

Back home I changed into something more comfortable and chilled out for a while. Strangely, the house seemed empty. Could I be missing Tom? Daytime television wasn't the answer so I called him. I mentioned that Alfie was sick and I was worried. We had a lengthy conversation and then I invited him to come round and make me a drink. He said he would and to expect him. It seemed that I had barely put the phone down when he was knocking on my door. Keen or what!

Something seemed different; he admitted that he'd been wrong. Tom had dropped his coat on the floor at the side of the sofa and Alfie immediately laid on it; she liked Tom and perhaps had been pining for him. Well, what's good enough for Alfie is good enough for me. Tom seemed genuinely sorry and maybe it had taken something like this to make him realise that he must allow me some space to live my life.

Friday 17th February 2006

I woke early and looked down at Tom as he lay sleeping. Had I done the right thing? I know I had said there would be no more chances but I did love him and I felt I owed him the benefit of any doubt I may still have.

We talked over breakfast I knew that I had done the right thing in letting him back into my life. Some people may disagree but that is not my problem. All I care about is the future and what it has in store. Tom said that his daughter had been disrupted by it all and would take some convincing that things were right between us. This concerned me as I liked his daughter but she will have to learn to live with it.

It was karaoke night but I was nervous about going to the Albert Hotel. How would people react to our on, off and on again relationship? I needn't have worried, no one bothered except the landlord who inquired what had happened between us. After I had explained, no more questions were asked. I was on form with my singing and really enjoyed myself.

Sunday 19th February 2005

Over the weekend Tom tried hard to make our relationship work. I don't want him to over do it but to just be himself, the person I fell in love with. His daughter came for Sunday lunch today. A potentially awkward situation did not happen and we had a wonderful day together.

Wednesday 22nd February 2006

Up until now things had been going well, then I developed a chest infection. My doctor prescribed the same medication that Tom has for his acne. Some days ago I began to develop ulcers on my body and my doctor is unhappy with me because these should have been treated sooner.

Thursday 23rd February 2006

I was dreading going shopping as I didn't feel well at all. I managed to carry on and go around town with Tom. OK, we had a laugh here and there about things but I couldn't wait to get home again. Back home I put the shopping away and did some washing. My body was telling me to stop and rest and I lay on the sofa and went to sleep. Eventually when I awoke, Tom was in a chair fast asleep so I gently roused him. When I asked how long we had been asleep he said he didn't know but he looked quite displeased. It was teatime and Tom was hungry. I said it would be easier for me to do frozen chips but his annoyance seemed to worsen. It's not often I don't feel like cooking but today was an exception. Tom knew I wasn't well so I hope he isn't trying to make me feel guilty again. Alfie seems to have gone downhill again, I'm really worried for her.

Friday 24th February 2006

The vet examined Alfie - she has colitis, which is treatable with antibiotics. Alfie was also weighed and I was amazed that she was over a stone. The vet gave me some advice about diet and at least I felt relieved that she had been seen by a professional and should be back to her normal self before long.

Later we went to the Albert Hotel. I was still expecting some questions about our brief "fall out" but no one bothered us. I sang lots of songs and drank alcohol free lager instead of boring fruit juice. It may be alcohol free, but at least I felt as though I'd had a proper drink.

I'm growing my hair long again so I booked an appointment to have it shaped. There is only one of the girls at the salon who understands my hair; she is the one who used to cut Daniel's hair. I'm a bit nervous of what it will look like but I have every confidence in her.

Tuesday 28th February 2006

Alfie is a lot better today although I must admit to feeling concerned last night. She had lost her appetite and was quite listless. However, my fears were groundless as Tom brought me the news that she was now eating again and seemed quite happy.

Today is my hair day. It didn't take as long as I thought it would. The hairdresser did a good job and I could feel the difference straight away.

Tuesday 14th March 2005

Over the past two weeks Alfie continued to improve and I also made an effort to get to know Tom's daughter much better. She really is a delightful young woman.

Friday 17th March 2006

Karaoke night at the Albert Hotel and I was in good voice. Midnight came and I still had two songs to do. It would have been my dad's birthday. There were others ahead of me in the queue so I asked if I could move my songs to the top of the list. The others didn't mind so I sang the remaining two songs for my dad. These were "The Wonder Of You" and "I Believe", both of which summed up my feelings for him. People began to dance; there was applause and whistles as I finished the last one. I felt happy and sad at the same time because, like Daniel, my dad is always close to me. It was well into Saturday morning before we arrived home.

Saturday 18th March 2005

At teatime I decided to call the D.J. from the Albert Hotel to see if he could get me a song that I once had in my collection. I'd always thought of my dad as a knight in shining armour and the song I wanted contained these words. He said he would try to get it for me. Not long afterwards he called me back to say he'd found it. The song is called "The Glory Of Love" and it is so special that I have memorized every word. He brought it to my house and I played it immediately.

I could see by Tom's face that he knew how much it meant to me. Later, as I turned the light off, I wished dad "happy birthday" and fell to sleep with the words of that song still buzzing round my brain.

Saturday 25th February 2006

Tomorrow will be Mothering Sunday and this will bring back memories. No matter how little Daniel had, even if he had to go into the garden and just pick something colourful for me, he would. Even though I knew that my other children would not send anything, every so often I found myself opening the door just hoping one of them may have sent a card or waiting for the phone to ring with that one call, but nothing came. I turned to Tom, telling him how I felt. He held me and I began to cry.

Sunday 26th February 2006

What should be a joyous day of celebration is full of pain for me. Tom's daughter is coming around for the day so I kept myself busy cooking Sunday lunch and doing some washing. Spring had finally shown it's face, the sun was shining and for the first time this year I had a chance to peg the washing out. I suppose I'm a bit old fashioned, watching freshly washed laundry blowing outside is such a pleasure.

Tom went to collect his daughter and the feelings of sadness returned. It wasn't jealousy but I thought to myself what did I ever do to deserve all the hurt. Tom had his daughter and I had no one. Surely my children are at an age when they should know that I would be hurting inside. At that moment, the door opened and Tom walked in with his daughter, she gave me a beautiful plant in a basket. Then she kissed me and said "Happy Mothers' Day". I held on to her so tightly, it was a special moment. She wasn't my own daughter but my feelings were just as intense. Her natural mother had died some time ago so this particular day gave both of us an opportunity to reach out and comfort each other.

It feels like this Mothering Sunday is a turning point. Hopefully, I have reached the end of my rainbow and found the pot of gold that I have been searching for – my new family. It is only now that I realise that I do not have to live behind a painted smile. I can show my face to the world and cope with whatever life has in store for me.

Thursday 1st March 2007

Tom is feeling quite ill today. He's passing a lot of blood in his urine so I ask him to make an appointment with the G.P. Typical Tom, he's reluctant to do this but I insist.

Saturday 3rd March 2007

Tom saw the doctor today and he is to have a scan. There is a waiting list so he will have to wait for two weeks.

Wednesday 7th March 2007

I've received an email that takes me by surprise. It contains a heading in capital letters - EMAIL NOTIFICATION AND FINAL NOTICE – very curious. It's from Yahoo Internet Lottery notifying me that I have won one million euros in a prize draw. In the email there's a batch number, lotto number and also a winning number. I was being congratulated; the email says that I must contact a fiduciary agent in Spain whose name is Mr. Fred Willington. Prominent within the email is a phone number so I telephone Spain to speak to the agent.

I am not a well off person, my disability prevents me from working and to be told that I have suddenly become rich just takes my breath away. It seems like forever but after a few rings someone answers the phone. I ask for the agent by name. A man confirms that he is Mr. Willington. He asks if I have a fax machine, as this will be the easiest and quickest way to exchange documents. He says that I need a passport to prove who I am. I tell him that I will go into town and purchase a fax machine and have a passport photograph taken. He tells me to call him back once I have installed the fax machine, which I agree to do.

He says he will fax me a document, which I must fill in. This document asks for personal details including bank account details and my next of kin. At this point he insists that I fax my passport photograph and the completed form to him. Again I comply.

Thursday 8th March 2007

I call the agent to see what I have to do next. I am instructed to stand by the fax machine as he is sending a certificate from Yahoo to confirm my win. A Dr. William Gerri, Lotto coordinator has signed the certificate. I have to call the agent when it arrives. Again I comply. The certificate looks genuine enough. I am advised to keep my win confidential because if it becomes public I will receive hundreds of begging letters. He says that he has been in meetings for most of the day with people from Yahoo about my award.

Friday 9th March 2007

I have been on the phone a lot today (at my expense) arranging things with the agent. He has explained the step-by-step procedure for the bank transfer and tomorrow he will be visiting the Ministry in Spain where a document will be issued to transfer the money from one country to another with it being such a large amount.

His secretary calls to say that he will be sending a fax. The document is from Ministerio de Justicia in Madrid. It even has an official looking stamp on it. It is all becoming too much for me to take in.

Saturday 10th March 2007

I am trying to make sense of everything that has happened over the past few days. I was told to phone Mr. Willington today. He said that to transfer the winnings into my bank account, the Spanish government requires that I send £1,754.00. Oh really, well maybe they do but I can't raise that kind of money. Mr. Willington tells me to stay calm and says he will speak with his wife to see if a loan can be arranged. He says his wife is on the other line and he will phone me later. When he contacts me it is to say that his wife can come up with £400.00 but I will still need to pay the balance. I begin to smell a rat.

Tuesday 13th March 2007

I phone Mr. Willington to tell him that I am unhappy and that I intend to call the Ministry in Spain. Instead I phone the police and book an appointment with my solicitor. The police are of the view that it is a case of identity theft. I am advised that if Mr. Willington persists with his phone calls I should hang up immediately and report it as soon as I can. The police say that this is the first time they have experienced this sort of thing done by email.

It is certainly one experience I wouldn't like to go through again. I feel such a fool being sucked in like this because I know that if I had had the money it would have been sent. People like Mr. Willington (if that's his real name) have no conscience; they don't care who they fleece or the damage they do to people who fall for their illegal con trick. This has been a lucky escape.

Saturday 17th March 2007

Tom had his scan today. He is very apprehensive but is hoping it will show what is wrong. It will be a month before he can see a consultant in urology.

Friday 13th April 2007

Today is Tom's appointment with the consultant. Because he's superstitious, Tom is not happy with the date - he knows the news won't be good. Waiting in reception is nerve wracking, then a nurse asks Tom to follow her into the consultant's office where he is told that he has cancer of the right kidney and it will have to be removed. Tom is calm about it and asks the consultant if he will need chemotherapy. The consultant replies that it won't be necessary. The consultant shows no emotion, it's just a job to him but I'm grateful that something is going to be done. Tom's operation was set for Thursday 19th April 2007 and he will be in hospital for 10 days. The consultant explains about the operation. Outside we talk about the arrangements that will have to be made.

Monday 16th April 2007

Tom is feeling dreadful. The operation is drawing nearer and it seems to be affecting him. I phone the hospital to ask if I could stay overnight on the evening before his operation. The answer is an abrupt "no", but I pack an overnight bag anyway. I generally don't take no for an answer. Transport will be a problem. I don't drive but I will have to visit Tom, so with cap in hand I ask John (my ex) if he will help. He is sorry to hear about Tom and said he'd take me four times, which may not cover the whole period of Tom's stay in hospital, but I am grateful for the gesture. For the rest of the time public transport won't work out so it will have to be taxis - an expensive business.

Wednesday 18th April 2007

Admission day. Although Tom slept well last night I didn't. There is too much floating round my head. The taxi is booked for 1 pm so we decide to go into town – anything is better than moping at home. The taxi arrives on time and off we go. I try to keep a conversation going but Tom seems to not hear me. The hospital has no plans to fast him until midnight so we go into the coffee shop. At least we can relax there.

At 7 pm Tom is quite nervous so I ask the sister in charge if I can stay the night. There are no facilities for this but I could sleep in a chair in the reception area. Tom is pleased and relieved that I'd be there for him in the morning. Well that's the plan but I have to live with the possibility that security might throw me out anyway. By now I'm feeling the pressure; my legs are giving way. Will all the stress bring on a fit – I hope not. I put on my painted smile and go into reception. The security guards understand my dilemma but I can't hold back the tears. A young receptionist makes me a cup of tea and a security guard tries to find me somewhere to stay.

At 10 pm a nurse says I can I sleep on a sofa in a spare room. I might not sleep too well but at least I will be comfortable.

Thursday 19th April 2007.

Operation day. I go to Tom's bedside and smile but inside I feel rotten. I really love this man and just pray that he will be alright. The porters help Tom onto a theatre bed. He is trembling with fear and my legs turn to jelly again. Tom's identity tag is checked as well as a few other things. I walk behind as they take him to theatre but I'm not allowed any further than the lift doors. He disappears from view and all I can do is wait.

Midday. A nurse tells me that Tom is out of theatre and in recovery. He'll be back in the ward at approximately 1.30 pm. I find a chair near the lift and wait there.

2 pm. At last – the lift doors open and there he is. The porters wheel him into the corridor and he manages to smile through his oxygen mask. I've never seen so many pipes and tubes but it was a major operation so that is to be expected. I say, "So you're back then?" Just like a man he asks for something to eat, but all he gets is 30 mls. of water. Tom is being monitored every thirty minutes. His progress is amazing.

8.30 pm. John arrives to take me home. It is good to be back in familiar surroundings. Never has a bath looked so inviting.

Friday 20th April 2007.

7.30 am. I've slept badly again. The house is empty without Tom. I phoned the ward and they tell me he is doing well.

11 am. John arrives and another day at the hospital lies ahead. Tom looks good considering what he's been through. Most of his tubes have gone. A nurse tells me that he's been drinking cups of tea and has had a pudding. Now there's a surprise! Even more of a surprise, he could be home on Monday. The nurses try him in a chair but he feels too much pain so they put him back to bed. He is given oral morphine. This stubborn man tries to deal with the pain himself but the operation was too extensive so he gives in to the nurses.

8.15 pm. Tom is still in some pain but it will ease in due course. I'm in reception waiting for John. The receptionist who had been kind to me is on duty and she shows an interest in how Tom is getting on. I thank her for the kindness and concern she is showing towards me. I can't help thinking what a great nurse she would make.

John arrives to take me home. Before going to bed at about 10.30 pm, I phone the ward and I'm told that Tom is sleeping; his pain must have eased.

Saturday 21st April 2007.

6.10 am. I've slept well for a change but I am feeling insecure not having Tom near me. I make a pot of tea and then launch into the ironing, hoping it will take my mind off things. Alfie my cat knows something is wrong. Tom isn't around to spoil her and she probably misses him just as much as I do.

7.00 am. I call the hospital. Tom has had a restful night so I'm feeling good about that.

11.30 am. John arrives and off I go to the hospital once again. I arrive to see Tom sitting up in bed wearing his own pyjamas for the first time. His wound drain is out and the number of clips holding him together shows the extent of the surgery.

1.30 pm. He tires quickly so I leave him to rest and go to the coffee shop next to which is a shop selling get well cards and other stuff. I buy a card, a get-well bear and a large balloon, which I leave behind the counter to collect when I've finished my lunch. Some people have short memories because the sales person had forgotten that I'd already paid for the balloon (no receipt) so I had to pay again or be accused of shoplifting.

8.50 pm. It's time to leave. I ask Tom to phone me when I get home. He didn't, so out of concern I call the ward. Tom had gone to sleep and the nurse reassures me that he is OK.

Sunday 22nd April 2007.

6.40 am. I'm wide-awake but won't be visiting Tom today. He understands that it's very tiring for me and because of my health problems I must not become exhausted.

8.00 am. Tom telephones me. His voice is full of pain and though he is up and about I know my place is with him. The problem is how do I get there? Taxi drivers charge the earth and my funds are limited.

I call a few friends without any luck. I'm becoming desperate. Tom needs me so I decide to do something that I may regret but I do it just the same. I phone my eldest sister. She recognises that I am genuinely in need of help and arranges for her son's wife to pick me up.

11.45 am. My lift has arrived. This is the first time I'd met my nephew's wife and we talked all the way to the hospital. It's strange really how adversity can bring out the best in people. Tom is surprised to see me but delighted just the same. We stand together looking out of the ward window. It's raining but the sun is out, a typical April day. Tom points to a rainbow; it must be a lucky omen. I remain unsure whether he is coming home tomorrow.

8.30 pm. My nephew and his wife are waiting to take me home. He's a sensible young man, just like Daniel would have been. Tom is healing and so is a part of my life that I thought was permanently damaged. I'm in bed by ten o'clock.

Monday 23ʳᵈ April 2007.

7.30 am. Up with the lark - I feel great. It's washday so everything goes in the machine. I won't be visiting Tom today. There is still a possibility he may be home later.

10.20 am. The phone rings, it's Tom, he's coming home but not until the nurses are sure that everything that should be working, is. He's to have some medication to start his bowels moving again.

3.30 pm. No movement yet – I've to ring back later.

5.20 pm. Still no movement – the medication isn't working but he can come home. If no bowel movement by tomorrow he has to "see someone". The love of my life is coming home even if his bowels aren't working. I can't wait.

7.15 pm. Tom arrives home. The stubborn man has carried his bag down the path. His face is full of pain. I shout for him to put the bag down, he shouldn't be carrying anything heavy. What is the hospital car driver thinking about allowing that to happen?

The hospital sent him home without any pain relief medication. How stupid is that? There is no overnight bag for his catheter either. He's in awful pain.

Prescription paracetamol has no effect. Tom is exhausted and looks dehydrated.

1.30 am. Tom is now really ill - he needs professional help. I call the out of hours surgery and receive reassurance that help is on the way.

1.40 am. I see car lights coming down the street. Two paramedics have arrived. I tell them about the absence of painkillers and the overnight catheter bag. One goes to the hospital, the other stays to help Tom.

2.15 am. The paramedic has returned with Tom's medication and an overnight bag. Tom is given three lots of painkillers - paracetamol, codeine and ibuprofen. I am instructed to get Tom some senna tablets the next day, as the codeine will constipate him further. That's all he needs!

2.40 am. Tom has settled.

Tuesday 24ᵗʰ April 2007.

3.00 pm. Sue, a district nurse has arrived to check on Tom and take some details. The paramedics have informed her of the problems relating to Tom's pain relief and catheter care. Tom is informed that a nurse will come on Sunday to remove his clips. Sue said that she had asked the hospital for information regarding Tom's operation. The hospital agreed to fax the details through but they have not arrived.

7.35 pm. I'm feeling angry. I phone the ward where Tom had been cared for and ask the sister for the nurse's name who had the responsibility for packing Tom's medication. She said Tom was only on paracetamol so I shouldn't worry. Just before he was discharged he'd been taking oral morphine so he will need something stronger than paracetamol. I stand my ground and the nurse's name is given to me. The sister tries to blame Tom. She says he should have checked that he had everything. That's a nurse's job, not Tom's. Then she says that everything had been done in a bit of a hurry. I reply that was no excuse and ring off.

8.00 pm. The ward sister phones me. She's full of apologies for the mistake and asks how Tom is getting on. I tell her that he is OK, no thanks to them. I said it's a pity that the same level of care and concern that he'd had in hospital had not been extended to his discharge.

10.00 pm. Tom is having a nightmare, screaming out "no, leave me alone". I gently shake him awake. He's having flashbacks to the operation. This happens again during the night.

Wednesday 25th April 2007.

6.15 am. Tom is much better today. He makes the tea but within minutes is back upstairs to use the bathroom. Thank goodness, the senna is working.

Thursday 26th April 2007.

It's shopping day. I settle Tom down then set out for town. It's odd having to do the shopping on my own but I manage it. My mobile doesn't ring so Tom must be OK.

Friday 27th April 2007.

Tom's in pain again this morning. He's run out of pain relief tablets and won't let me call anyone. I ignore him and phone the surgery for a prescription. He soon settles once the tablets take effect.

Saturday 28th April 2007.

A better day, that is until Tom's catheter bag bursts. His clothes are saturated. Putting a new one on is a bit tricky but between us we manage. I wash Tom's soiled clothes – it's a good drying day thank goodness.

Sunday 29ᵗʰ April 2007.

11.45 am. Tom is a bit agitated. The nurse is supposed to be here to take his clips out but she is late. He is worried that she might come during lunchtime.

12.55 pm. The nurse is here now and she removes Tom's clips. He is still a bit tender round the site of his operation. The clips come out so fast that poor Tom does not have time to draw breath. The nurse says that the hospital has not contacted her yet about Tom's operation. It really isn't good enough.

5.00 pm. Tom is in pain again. He is trying to cough but this puts a strain on his operation wound. It's awful watching him, I feel helpless. I fetch a glass of water and tell him to take tiny sips. This seems to help. He says he feels as if his insides have been pulled apart.

Tuesday May 1ˢᵗ 2007.

Tom has an appointment with his consultant today. John picks us up early and we arrive at the hospital two hours before the appointment time. Thank goodness for the coffee shop.

11.15 am. A nurse calls Tom into the clinic. She removes his catheter, which is a great relief. This time it is a painless procedure. He then performs two flow rate tests to see if he is passing urine freely. Everything is OK.

12.15 pm. The consultant calls Tom in to see him. I go with him. We are told that Tom's cancer has gone. The consultant says that it was a transitional cell carcinoma and it had been confined to the kidney. Tom will need regular check ups at three monthly intervals. These will be arranged at a hospital nearer to where we live. We shake the consultant's hand and thank him for everything.

Wednesday May 2nd 2007.

Tom is restless. He wants to run before he can walk. I tell him the gardening can wait, he has to take it easy for quite a long time, but we know that we have our lives back again. Thank God for that.

EPILOGUE

All I can hope for now is that Tom's cancer has been completely cured. He has brought so much contentment and happiness to my life. Although the horrors of my past will always be with me, they are fading and with Tom's love to support me I have a strong feeling that together we can look towards the sun and build a positive and fulfilling life together.

ABOUT THE AUTHOR ——————

When I first began to write, I found a new meaning, that life really is what you make it. Such as I cannot talk to people about my problems. However, I can share them by writing for people to read. Being able to write is something that I had never considered doing, until I sat down one evening with an A4 writing pad and found that once I had began I could not stop. The words just seem to come naturally, and in the process it helped me to overcome so many things that have happened in my life. I can honestly say that to begin with I was not certain about all the 'limelight' that comes with being an author. However, I think that I have gone past that stage now, where people recognized me in the street and asked, if I am "that author?" I have had people asking if I have had a writing course, the answer is no. All that I write does come straight from the heart, all my emotions and feelings wrapped into one. I must say that I enjoy writing more than anything else, I just wished that I had done it sooner. The feedback that I have had previously has been tremendous. If I had the chance to do it all again I would. If by writing, means it can help not just myself but other people too, then it would have all been worthwhile.

Lightning Source UK Ltd.
Milton Keynes UK
UKOW02f1201051114

241113UK00007B/5/A